Citizen Journalism
as Conceptual Practice

Frontiers of the Political

Series Editor:

Engin Isin is Professor of International Politics, Queen Mary University of London (QMUL) and University of London Institute in Paris (ULIP). He is a leading scholar of citizenship studies and is a Chief Editor of the journal *Citizenship Studies*. He is author and editor of eleven books in the field, including *Being Political* and *Citizens Without Frontiers*.

This series aims to contribute to our understanding of transversal political struggles beyond and across the borders of the nation-state, and its institutions and mechanisms, which have become influential and effective means of both contentious politics and political subjectivity. The series features titles that eschew and even disavow interpreting these transversal political struggles with categories and concepts.

Postcolonial Transitions in Europe: Contexts, Practices and Politics
edited by Sandra Ponzanesi and Gianmaria Colpani

Citizenship and Place: Case Studies on the Borders of Citizenship
edited by Cherstin M. Lyon and Allison F Goebel

The Question of Political Community: Sameness, Logos, Space
by Jonna Pettersson

Postcolonial Intellectuals in Europe: Academics, Artists, Activists and Their Publics
edited by Sandra Ponzanesi and Adriano José Habed

*Citizen Journalism as Conceptual Practice: Postcolonial Archives and
Embodied Political Acts of New Media*
by Bolette B. Blaagaard

Governing Affective Citizenship: Denaturalisation, Belonging and Repression
by Marie Beauchamps

Citizen Journalism as Conceptual Practice

Postcolonial Archives and Embodied Political Acts of New Media

Bolette B. Blaagaard

London • New York

Published by Rowman & Littlefield International, Ltd.
6 Tinworth Street, London SE11 5AL, United Kingdom
www.rowmaninternational.com

Rowman & Littlefield International Ltd. is an affiliate of Rowman & Littlefield
4501 Forbes Boulevard, Suite 200, Lanham, Maryland 20706, USA
With additional offices in Boulder, New York, Toronto (Canada), and Plymouth (UK)
www.rowman.com

Selection and editorial matter © Bolette B. Blaagaard, 2018

Paperback edition published 2020

All rights reserved. No part of this book may be reproduced in any form or by any electronic or mechanical means, including information storage and retrieval systems, without written permission from the publisher, except by a reviewer who may quote passages in a review.

British Library Cataloguing in Publication Data
A catalogue record for this book is available from the British Library

ISBN: HB 978-1-78660-107-0
ISBN: PB 978-1-78660-108-7

Library of Congress Cataloging-in-Publication Data

Names: Blaagaard, Bolette, author.
Title: Citizen journalism as conceptual practice : postcolonial archives and embodied political acts of new media / Bolette B. Blaagaard.
Description: London ; New York : Rowman & Littlefield International, Ltd., [2018] | Series: Frontiers of the political | Includes bibliographical references.
Identifiers: LCCN 2018005954 (print) | LCCN 2018008540 (ebook) | ISBN 9781786601094 (electronic) | ISBN 9781786601070 (cloth : alk. paper) | ISBN 9781786601087 (paper : alk. paper)
Subjects: LCSH: Citizen journalism. | Postcolonialism. | Journalism—Technological innovations.
Classification: LCC PN4784.C615 (ebook) | LCC PN4784.C615 B57 2018 (print) | DDC 070.4/3—dc23
LC record available at https://lccn.loc.gov/2018005954

Figure C.1   David Hamilton Jackson speaking at Grønttorvet, Copenhagen, 1915.
Reprinted courtesy of The Danish Royal Library.

Contents

List of Figures		ix
Acknowledgements		xi
1	Shifting Perspectives: Understanding Citizen Journalism through a 'Politics of Location'	1
2	Deconstructing the Citizen Journalist	23
3	Political Citizen Journalism: Cosmopolitanism and Citizenship in Colonies	45
4	Embodied Citizen Journalism: Archives and Postcolonial Memory	65
5	Citizen Journalism and the Politics of Visibility	89
6	Conclusions: Citizen Journalism as an Act for Transformation	107
Bibliography		119
Index		125
About the Author		131

List of Figures

Figure C.1	David Hamilton Jackson speaking at Grønttorvet, Copenhagen, 1915	v
Figure 4.1	Page 2 of *The Herald*, 8 March 1916	78
Figure 4.2	Front page of *The Herald*, 3 July 1917	82

Acknowledgements

I would like to thank colleagues and friends for insightful and helpful comments on drafts of this book's chapters. Some of the chapters are based on previously published articles and chapters, and I would like to thank the reviewers and editors for their work. I would like to thank the Danish Royal Library and the National Archives, my friends and colleagues in the United States Virgin Islands, as well as the team at Rowman & Littlefield for their collaboration and interest in the project. Finally, I thank Rosi Braidotti for her continued support and friendship. This book is dedicated to Johannes Benjamin.

Parts of chapters 2, 3 and 4 have been published in:

'Cosmopolitan relations in the colonies: Redefining citizen journalism through a cultural historical reading of *The Herald*, St. Croix 1915–25', *European Journal of Cultural Studies* (2016), 1–17.

'Reading *The Herald* today: Postcolonial notes on journalism and citizen media', in Sandra Ponzanesi and Gianmaria Colpani (eds.), *Postcolonial Transitions in Europe: Contexts, Practices and Politics* (Lanham, MD: Rowman & Littlefield, 2016), 231–50.

Rosi Braidotti and Paul Gilroy, 'Questions of memory and cosmopolitan futures of Europe', in Sandra Ponzanesi and Adriano Habed (eds.), *Postcolonial Intellectuals in Europe: Academics, Artists, Activists and Their Publics* (Lanham, MD: Rowman & Littlefield, 2018).

1

Shifting Perspectives

Understanding Citizen Journalism through a 'Politics of Location'

> Theory – the seeing of patterns, showing the forest as well as the trees – theory can be a dew that rises from the earth and collects in the rain cloud and returns to earth over and over. But if it doesn't smell of the earth, it isn't good for the earth.
>
> —Adrienne Rich, 'Notes towards a Politics of Location', 213–14

In 1984, Adrienne Rich wrote 'Notes towards a Politics of Location', in which she argues for a grounded approach to theoretical work. Behind its lyrical wording, the above quote suggests an understanding of knowledge production that takes both its starting point and raison d'être in a grounded cartographic reading of particular circumstances. These particular circumstances give life to concepts, which in turn allow for a new understanding of the practice that served as the initial starting point. Similarly, in his work on cinema, Deleuze argues, 'A theory about cinema is not "about" cinema but about the concepts that cinema generates' (Deleuze 1989, 280). Inspired by Rich and Deleuze, I argue in this book that citizen journalism is not about citizen journalism but about citizens and journalism as well as about how these concepts and practices formulate and generate political practices of subjectivity formation. Deleuze sees cinema as a practice of knowledge production on par with philosophical knowledge production, though generated through different events and understandings. I do not argue that citizen journalism is a philosophy but rather that looking at citizen journalism as a particular practice of knowledge production with a historical presence allows us to understand more about its role in society and about subjects' political practices and agency. In arguing this, I furthermore draw upon philosophy of subjectivity, postcolonial theory, theories of citizenship and theories of political acts in order to take a new perspective on citizen journalism. This enables me to move beyond binary positions often evoked in empirical discussions about citizen journalism, such as the amateur producer of news versus the professional journalist, the importance of technological developments versus cultural determinism and the particular versus universal expressions. In other words, I wish to move to a position situated outside the dichotomies established by previous studies and long-held beliefs regarding an opposition between the practices of citizen journalism and professional journalism, which remain determining factors and points of reference. I wish to question the role and meaning of the 'citizen' and the mnemonic processes, positions and substance of 'journalism' when discussing citizen journalism.

In order to shift perspective on citizen journalism from a focus on journalistic practice to a focus on processes of subjectivity, I consider the case of a colonial newspaper which was published in St. Croix between 1915 and 1925 by a descendant of enslaved people in this colony within the Danish West Indies. I read this newspaper, *The Herald*, to develop my perspective for three reasons: First, as a case of colonial citizens' communication through a journalistic medium, it challenges the perceived boundaries of the nation-state on which professional journalism and the idea of the citizen are predicated. This is further amplified by the precarity experienced by the populations of St. Croix, St. John and St. Thomas, when these islands were sold to the United States in 1917. Despite expectations to the contrary, the sale did not immediately result in US citizenship for the islands' inhabitants but instead initiated a new struggle for civil rights, one that continues in the US Virgin Islands to this day. Second, the historical location of the case releases us from the digital saturation of debates on citizen journalism long enough to refocus on the material, actual public and its embodied and situated space. Debates about digital expressions and participation have suggested a particular kind of democratisation through digital media through an expansion of the public sphere. The space of the postcolonial, however, demonstrates the limits of the public sphere as a concept and highlights the need for an analysis of power. Finally, the particular circumstances surrounding *The Herald* are important. *The Herald* invites a close reading of its ten years of publication and archived storage, which represents a counter-reading of both journalism history and Danish (colonial) history. The founder and editor of the paper, David Hamilton Jackson, was a descendant of enslaved people, who agitated for the rights of the islands' labourers to better wages and shorter working weeks. I argue that the racialized political conditions on the islands (as well as in interaction with Denmark and the United States' mainland) allow us to revisit our reading of the journalistic practice of Jackson and his peers in a manner that underscores their call for equal rights and social awareness as crucial to the practice of citizen journalism. Citizen journalism can be regarded as a conceptual practice not just because of its mechanics but also because of its grounding and meaning-making ability. By deconstructing the relationships between citizen journalism, the journalistically understood and amplified public sphere, and the nationally and politico-legally bound idea of the citizen, I highlight the importance of *The Herald* and Jackson's journalistic political and embodied practice. *The Herald* of St. Croix, 1915–1925, thus allows me to answer – in my view – far more interesting questions than 'What is citizen journalism?': 'How may we understand the concept of the citizen in citizen journalism?' 'From which kinds of politics and social community may this citizen's journalism arise?' 'What kinds of politics can it create?'

The relationship between the colonial groundings of citizen journalism and the theoretical implications of a politics of location generates questions of subjectivity formation and political agency. This book thus has three interlinked theoretical aims: (1) It aims to bring about a new reading of citizen journalism that focusses on the practice of producing political citizenship and subjectivity formations. I therefore understand practice as actively producing material subjectivities. (2) It aims to analytically argue that our understanding of citizen journalistic subjectivity formation is enhanced through (post)colonial perspectives and positions but that these perspectives and positions are hard-earned modalities of constant learning. (3) Finally, this book aims to shed new light on the relationship between journalism – understood in broad terms rather than in terms of a profession – and subjectivity, with special emphasis on ethical and political accountability. In short, this book argues that citizen journalism, if understood as a political process of subjectivity, has the capacity for social change that encompasses another (concept of the) public and citizenship based on new ethico-political relations and new grounded experiences.

Whereas chapter 2 will delve deeper into issues of citizenship and public participation, this first chapter further develops my approach to citizen journalism and focusses on the relationship between theories inspired by Deleuze and the colonial groundings of citizen journalism. After a short introduction to scholarship in the field under the heading 'What Is Citizen Journalism?', I shift towards an understanding of citizen journalism as necessarily historically and geographically situated, embodied in countercultural positions and political beyond the participatory. The chapter continues by returning to the Deleuzian inspiration in the section 'Deleuze on Conceptual Personae and Practice: A Politics of Location', in which I discuss my use of concept and conceptual practice, including theorisation of the Deleuzian and Guattarian conceptual personae and practice. This approach is then reworked through engagement with Rosi Braidotti's analytical idea and approach to politics of location, which is, moreover, inspired by the work of Rich. These two methodological groundings – of the conceptual practice and of politics of location – mark a shift in philosophical thinking that emphasises multiplicity and multilayered analyses in contrast to approaches structured around binary, teleological and typological categorisations. The chapter proceeds by juxtaposing the perspectives of conceptual practice and politics of location with work by postcolonial scholars on the political and representational asymmetry of the voices and bodies of (post)colonial peoples and sites. In the section 'Spivak and Onwards: Postcolonial Reflections', I address the interactions between Deleuze and postcolonial theory, and in the section 'Braidotti on the Deterritorialization of Identity', I extend my proposed application of the intersections between Deleuzian and postcolonial theories on citizen journalism. Postcolonial theories and readings have received little attention in Deleuzian thought, despite the two traditions' shared critique of universalism and Eurocentrism, their similar methods, and their focus on defamiliarization and disrupting the given (Braidotti 2011). The chapter argues, however, for the importance of a postcolonial reading of citizen journalism from a *longue durée* perspective, combined with grounded reading against the grain, in order to conceptualise citizen journalism in a manner that permits a fuller understanding of this shifting and developing field. Gayatri Spivak (1988) denounced Foucault and Deleuze for failing to acknowledge the political and representational asymmetries in their work on otherness and subjectivity. In this chapter, I discuss Spivak's quarrel with certain aspects of poststructuralist thinking and argue for a necessary and fruitful collaboration between these theoretical frameworks.

WHAT IS CITIZEN JOURNALISM?

In this book, I move from the current conceptualisation of citizen journalism as a practice that is opposed to professional journalism and driven by technological developments. These conceptualisations of citizen journalism are often developed through empirical investigations within media and journalism studies and focus on the implications of citizen journalism for professional journalism. The term 'citizen journalism' is presented as having its origins with the tsunami that washed over Southeast Asia in 2004 (Allan 2009, 2011), when bystanders shot and disseminated footage of the disaster that they recorded on their mobile devices. Citizen journalism is sometimes said to have entered the mental and global stage, if not the vocabulary, as early as the 1990s, when internet user participation started generating gossip and alternative news online (Rojas and Kim 2008, Friedland and Kim 2009). In the scholarship, citizen journalism covers such diverse practices as blogging; recording and disseminating mobile phone footage and images; and spreading and sharing debates through online platforms, networks or mainstream news sites. These diverse usages broaden the scope and frameworks of citizen journalism, yet the eclectic and changeable nature of the empirical data being examined blurs the term's theoretical focus. By examining the conceptual practice or processes of understanding that are produced through citizen journalism, I argue for a shift in perspectives. I begin by briefly outlining dominant perspectives. I do not attempt exhaustive coverage of either journalism studies or citizen journalism (for an overview of the latter, see Wall 2015) but instead present a few points of reference that will guide this book's argument. In the following, I identify two major axes around which many debates concerning different definitions of citizen journalism revolve: participation and technology.

Although the origins and usage of 'citizen journalism' remain unclear, the term is now a staple in companions to and encyclopaedias of journalism (Sterling 2009), social movements studies (Downing 2011), political science (Kaid and Holtz-Bacha 2008) and citizen media (Pérez-González, Blaagaard and Baker forthcoming 2019). The range of fields within which the term is present is indicative of its interdisciplinary use and political reach. In these companion and encyclopaedia entries, citizen journalism is often connected to the practices of civic journalism and participatory journalism (see also Singer et al. 2011), which focus on the civic involvement of professional journalism in communities and hark back to the classic texts on public engagement through the press by John Dewey and Walter Lippmann (see also Allan 2012). Dewey and Lippmann had opposing views on how journalism should engage with and inform the public, and it is often argued that Dewey's emphasis on journalism taking its cue from the people and community has gained credibility in today's online debates. Lippmann's warning about the falling quality and lack of independence in journalistic work and the resultant lack of trust in media representations is, however, likewise pertinent and is frequently deployed in discussions concerning citizen journalism's impact on professional journalism. This discourse grants an ambiguous role to citizen journalism as both a certifier of authentic truth dealt by the non-partisan bystander and citizen participant and as a threat to the journalistic ideal of objectivity and independence. The focus on the participating bystander or citizen is further elaborated upon when citizen journalism is theorised as 'witnessing' (Allan 2013, Frosh and Pinchevski 2011). Allan uses the term 'citizen witnessing' to offer an alternative perspective to professional journalism's public service and understands technological developments as enabling new journalistic democratic cultures (Allan 2013, 20–21). In contrast, Frosh and Pinchevski regard media witnessing as a perpetual self-affirmation in which the audience is both addressee and producer, continually reflecting itself and witnessing its own shared world (2011, 11–12). The concept of the witness moreover introduces the physicality and affectivity of the body. The witness is presented as the ultimate citizen journalist: the alternative, embodied eyes on a newsworthy situation. The witness gives a partial look – if not a partisan look – at the news and political events on a global scale, but this is precisely what is attractive about these citizens' reports: their 'authenticity' as opposed to the 'objectivity' of journalistic reports (Blaagaard 2013, Wahl-Jørgensen 2012). The concepts of the witness and testimony provide fertile ground for thinking about the value and documentation of 'the truth' in journalists' and citizens' engagements alike. The relationship between the witness's memory and the recorded and documented (historical) truth is framed not only by the archive but also, as I argue in chapter 3, by the newspaper. Moreover, both collective memory and national forgetfulness are pivotal to understanding citizenship and rights claims. Leaving aside for the present the intricate interweaving of memory, journalistic witnessing and citizenship, suffice it say that citizen journalism may be understood as a practice that stands in relation to professional journalism, either as a critique of professional journalism's inability to capture the hearts and minds of everyday people or as a means of entering into the public arena and engaging with the public discussion that is framed and interpreted by the professional journalistic institutions. As such, citizen journalism simultaneously serves as an alternative to and as a developing position within the public arena governed by journalistic institutions and news media logic. Citizen journalism is thus presented as a natural movement towards universal participation, supported by a free press. It is the next and inevitable step in social and democratic development, yet it is also ambiguous and problematic, as evidenced by studies of state and corporate surveillance and control (Tufekci 2014, Dencik, Hintz and Cable 2016). The understanding of citizen journalism as a development of participation in the public sphere may simultaneously support a narrative in which the affectivity and authenticity of citizen journalism prove vexing.[1]

Citizen journalism's participatory position within a public sphere, as advanced by some journalism and social media scholarship, is made possible through technology. Another axis of debate that emerges out of readings concerning the term 'citizen journalism' thus involves the influence of digitalisation and technology. Citizen journalism's connection to technology is not limited to the rise of the internet but can be traced back to earlier technological developments. Gillmor (2004) suggests that the liberation from the postal service stamp tax in the nineteenth-century United States and the subsequent proliferation of the journalistic market may represent a forerunner of citizen journalism. Not only did cheaper paper production, availability of the printing press and lower taxes enable a surge in publication of pamphlets and journals, but telegraph technology helped spread local and specific news between distant regions, thereby virtually bringing together the individual states and supporting an imagined community (Schudson 2003, Carey 1992, Gonzales and Torres 2011, Anderson 1991) of a unified (and) United States. Telegraphed reports were paid for by the word, resulting in reports that were short and to the point. This, Carey (1992) believes, further limited bias in the language of late nineteenth- and early twentieth-century journalistic reports. Technology may thus historically be seen as supporting objectivity by helping to regulate human biases expressed through florid adjectives and long opinion pieces, leading to a foregrounding of rational argumentation.

This idea, however, that journalistic objectivity was born partly in tandem with the technology of the wire and the necessity of political communication through technology has now been thoroughly discussed (see Schudson and Anderson 2009, Wahl-Jørgensen 2012) and disputed, if not completely rejected. While the notion that technology and journalism (and concomitantly, citizen journalism) combine to enable and sustain political and social culture, in the past as well as today, remains prevalent in journalism studies and studies of social media, this view can only be upheld when global connectivity is understood solely in terms of democratic enhancement and with a firm belief in human rationality and ideal ability of argumentation. Bearing in mind the digital, economic, gendered, racialized and cultural divides traversing the internet (Curran, Fenton and Freedman 2012); the commercialisation of private lives (van Dijck 2013); and online hate speech and trolling, citizen journalism cannot be regarded as shattering the co-dependency of technology and objectivity. Citizen journalism can instead be seen as offering public debates not only rational but also affective and creative interjections that are enhanced and enabled by technology. Such considerations seem too overwhelming to neglect. I seek to take a citizens' perspective (rather than a public sphere perspective) on the complex interactions and power struggles between citizens' and corporations' social and cultural positions as well as the political hegemony of journalistic ideals and values. Given that racial, economic and social divides persist, I wish to ask: 'Who can be considered a citizen journalist? Who is listened to and therefore able to appear in public?' This, I argue, is not just a matter of access and participation but is also inevitably connected to issues of power and the struggle to carve out a public on one's own terms. These questions clearly mirror the question of who counts as 'human', a question that postcolonial studies as well as poststructuralism's post-humanism and new humanism have sought to query. It is also a question with which media studies has engaged in its explorations of whose voices are considered worth listening to and whose experiences are deemed relatable (see for instance Silverstone 2007, Couldry 2010, Chouliaraki 2013a).

It is important to note that the axes of debates set forth above are primarily based on teleological understandings of citizen journalism and the citizen journalist. The Dewey–Lippmann debate and the technological leaps of the telegraph and printing press are both sustained by a linear argument in which citizen journalism developed as a part of the mediatisation process that influenced politics, geography, economy and culture. Indeed, the partly private–partly public online societal participation through the latest media technology available may be understood as a result of the mediatisation process of our daily lives. Citizen journalism is, then, just the most recent practice inferred by this process and one through which the conditions of our media lives and practices are continuously transforming (Couldry 2008, Silverstone 2007). This approach develops theory and conclusions from one empirical event to the next, involving the affected citizens as citizen journalists: social uprising, political scandal, natural disaster, technological invention or new practice – all allow us to think and conclude anew about what citizen journalism is and who citizen journalists are. An empiricist approach will then enable a new description and a new explanation of the particular events and the importance of the related media to society. With every event, we learn more about what citizen journalism could also be and who is allowed to produce it: The next step in a social and political development through communication technology. However, given the overwhelmingly white, English-speaking and affluent demographic to which the researchers in the field (this author included) and the key texts belong and our tendency to research accessible populations (often similar to ourselves), it is necessary to consider that the field may produce a skewed image of the citizen journalist (Neumayer and Rossi 2016).

A recent return to theory and to ethnographic research has prompted changes in the field of citizen journalism. For instance, the work of Clemencia Rodríguez (2011) focusses on citizens' media as practices and uses of media technology. Through extensive ethnographic work in war-torn Colombia, she shows how 'small media' are utilised as points of resistance in regions of conflict. Rodríguez insists on using the term 'citizens' media' rather than 'citizen journalism' or 'citizen media' in order to ground her theories in citizens' actual, material practices. Rodríguez (2011) argues that citizen media should be thought of as neither assets, as means of helping Westernized media institutions, nor as tools for disseminating public service announcements. Rather, citizen media are instead community-building practices, engaging their participants in multiple and grounded ways. This approach is in line with a postcolonial critique of Western-centric ethics, structures and functions of media (Rao and Wasserman 2007). In a similar vein, the collected volume of investigations into *Citizen Media and Public Spaces* (Baker and Blaagaard 2016) diverges from preconceptions about citizen media and journalism by emphasising the importance of physical spaces and political environments to citizens' expressions. In terms of digital media, there have also been critical perspectives on the role that social media and corporate control play in citizen journalism, as yet another institutionalisation of freedom of speech and a free press (Fuchs 2014, van Dijck and Poell 2014). Notwithstanding the differences in defining citizens' media, citizen media and citizen journalism, their material and digital surroundings and ability to restrict or enable political communication in given communities are clearly of fundamental importance to these studies' definition of citizens' political and public engagements through media practices. This means that they all depart from the approach that has long dominated journalism studies.

Partly following the sentiments drawn from these new approaches and investigations, this book argues that inquiry into the nature of citizen journalism requires us to simultaneously think through particular practices and develop a theory of citizen journalism as a process of subjectivity formation. 'Who is a citizen journalist?' and 'What is citizen journalism?' are questions that depend upon concepts and subjectivities arising from the particular practice. Their answers are, moreover, dependent upon the vision or idea of the historical, economic and social developments within which this political practice through journalism has moved. They also require a keen eye on other possible narratives and events: not as historical events confined within their historicity but as grounded and meaning-making events. The question of who counts and has historically counted as a citizen or indeed as a human being must be invoked to understand the dynamics and processes of citizen journalism as conceptual practice.

The shift in perspectives for which I am arguing thus involves moving away from a definition of citizen journalism as technologically enhanced participation to a definition that stems from a grounded theoretical approach to citizens' political acts generated through media.

SITUATED, EMBODIED, POLITICAL

I have previously addressed the special challenges posed by citizen journalism, not only in relation to professional journalism but also – and more importantly – in terms of how the practice may help us rethink the relationship between public space and political communication (Blaagaard 2013). Based on case studies research, I grouped diverse products of citizen journalism into three different kinds of expressions: the crisis reporting, the political issue and the visual debate. Whereas crisis reporting may be a product of the bystander being in the right place at the right time, this kind of citizen journalism could also represent a political statement: a deliberate view from inside the policed 'kettle' at European anti-austerity demonstrations or from the deserted, bombed-out cities of Syria. Crisis reporting could be said, then, to be a question of 'voice' (Couldry 2010, Chouliaraki 2013b) as well as of 'witnessing' (Allan 2013). As such, crisis reporting requires embodied presence and that it is situated in a particular event or community. Citizen journalism expressions that focussed on a particular political issue are more overtly or traditionally political but retain a belief in the necessity of showing the other side of the story: This group is oppositional by definition and supports the production of a counterpublic (Fraser 1990, Warner 2002). Finally, visual debates focus on the dialogical and visual aspects of this group of citizen journalist expressions as they occur on digital content-sharing platforms such as YouTube (see also van Zoonen, Vis and Mihelj 2010). I found this last group of citizen journalism expressions to be embodied. It could be argued that what is at stake here are various aspects or modalities of the expression of citizen journalism – rather than distinct groups of citizen journalism – as it presents itself and the world in present-day technological public space. The expressions seemed to share a rational form of communication. New media allows citizen journalists to contextualise and situate the news from personal and political perspectives and with a bodily experience to back up their contributions. It thereby challenges the abstract and analytical conceptualisation of publicness, reshaping the relationship between the public and the private in civil society and challenging journalistic objectivity and mainstream media representation (Blaagaard 2013, 197).

These three modalities of citizen expressions (the situatedness and political and embodied expression) will be explored and theorised in relation to the colonial newspaper *The Herald* in this book's three analytical chapters in which I produce a cartography of citizen journalism through readings of *The Herald*. By positioning itself in opposition to, relation to or in dialogue with a public, *The Herald*'s citizen journalism addresses a public and brings it into existence through circulating discourse. Citizen journalism is thus arguably a political act of citizenship (e.g., Isin and Nielsen 2008, Isin and Ruppert 2015).

Bearing in mind the situated character of citizen journalism, in chapter 3, I review the (post)colonial and journalistic times in which *The Herald* was published and argue that, despite existing historical reviews of the emergence of professional journalism, which took place around the time of *The Herald*'s publication in the early years of the twentieth century, professional journalistic practice and particularly the practice of objectivity looks somewhat different when viewed from the perspective of the African American and Caribbean press. I underscore the importance of *The Herald*'s political content, which helped produce a sense of citizenship in the colony. Rather than simplifying journalistic language and thereby producing a neutral and shortened, to-the-point, report, as Carey argued (1992), the telegraph streamlined white racist views and helped roll back civil rights gained by the African American population in the preceding years (González and Torres 2011). In contrast to the pursuit of faux objectivity, the African American press, as well as *The Herald*, favoured a personal and political writing style that openly argued for improving the conditions of the African American population. Chapter 3 shows that, on the one hand, the traditional narrative of the professionalization of journalistic practice is Eurocentric and universalistic and, on the other hand, citizen journalism as a political act potentially possesses an alternative history rooted in (post)colonial struggles for civil rights rather than in the twenty-first century's technologically nurtured revolutions of the Middle East and Arab states and the 'war on terror'.

Chapter 4 advances the in-depth cartographic reading of *The Herald*, this time with a focus on embodiment and the political use of memory and history in both *The Herald* and in the archives that hold and produce the political realm in which *The Herald* exists. The analysis in chapter 4 helps to draw out the processes underlying citizen journalism as a historically embodied witness. The chapter begins by theorising how mnemonic devices produce subjectivity – including political subjectivity – in postcolonial and poststructuralist thinking. It then goes on to analyse two particular entries in *The Herald* in which the embodiment of the citizen witness as a historical presence creates political acts through its distinct, historically and experientially grounded format. The editorial articles analysed in this chapter are engagements by Jackson with the history of the public which he addressed. As such, they may be seen as events or gestures, repeatable but changing. These two editorials are written at two distinct times in the history of *The Herald*, the islands and the African Caribbean public, and they draw upon two documenting texts that relate to *The Herald* and to the colonial situation in significantly different ways. Drawing upon the work of thinkers such as Rosi Braidotti, the analysis shows how Jackson uses memory to reinforce the political act as well as to address a public beyond his paper's readership through a shared history of enslavement and struggle. However, the analysis also illustrates the limits to memory, arguing for the importance of embodiment and situatedness in engaging with the creative power of re-membering. The structure of the editorials represents a gesture that, through repetition, highlights the 'changing same' (Gilroy 1994) of embodied expressions.

In chapter 5, I return to current discussions, presenting and discussing the postcolonial and critical perspectives relative to the political act in today's visually saturated public space of digital media. This chapter focusses on the visual political act of today's citizen journalism and argues that, like texts, images may be produced as either participatory acts (within an established public) or as political acts that disrupt the visuality (Mirzoeff 2011) of contemporary politics. All three expressions or aspects of citizen journalism – the situated, embodied and political – relate to a different concept of the public than that which Jürgen Habermas (1989) and theorists following his lead developed and grounded in humanism. Although the dialogical focus of the visual expressions may speak to the notion of deliberative engagement and discursive ethics, the notion of showing the other side, of standing in opposition, is ultimately agonistic. As a result, I introduce Mirzoeff's radical reworking of Arendt's 'space of appearance' and read it against the structural and regulatory visuality of iconic imagery in media (Hariman and Lucaites 2011) in a politics of visibility based on exclusions and inclusions. Here, Michael Warner's (2002) theoretical exploration of the concepts of the public, publics and counterpublics may serve as an entry point. While *the* public is a totality based on the exclusion of an Other, to Warner, *a* public emerges through an address. However, not just any address will do: The address must bring into existence a community or public through an answer to the call – a participation. Mirzoeff's space of appearance insists on forging a space that, like Warner's publics, is a self-organising, reflexive space of social interaction and discursive circulation and is moreover a material act of political struggle. For Warner, rather than being framed by an external structure, a public is constituted and upheld by people engaging in a discourse. A public is thus a process of continuous recirculation and citation, framed independently of national or ethnic borders. In chapter 5, this theorisation is tested through analyses of images of protesters at Black Lives Matter demonstrations in the United States as an example of mediated and embodied civil rights struggles today.

Belonging to a particular public is not simply given by birth or by identity but involves participation in the recirculation of discourse, says Warner. Publics encompass all who participate. Warner uses 'participation' in a very broad sense, in which simply paying attention suffices. Such publics, based on a bare minimum of participation, must encompass both personal and impersonal relations as well as relations to strangers (Warner 2002, Blaagaard and Roslyng 2016). It may be argued that such a broad concept of participation risks pandering to the slacktivist and the cynic (Morozov 2011). It may also be argued that it risks neglecting the implications of online and mainstream media institutions' corporate power (Fuchs 2014). While these critiques are valid and important, they also stifle the political capabilities of everyday people. Seeking a middle ground, I wish to analyse and understand citizen journalism as a practice and, more importantly, as a material act of addressing a public. I thereby employ a cartographic strategy for grounding political engagement through counter-readings or ways of thinking against the grain of dominant social representations (Braidotti 2011, 271). This does not mean ignoring the political realities of corporate power and neo-pragmatic attitudes; it instead means engaging with these as part of the diverse and traversing movements that comprise the cartography of the practice. This approach makes it appropriate to discuss the historical formations of discursive publics and identifications through technologies of memory and archivization.

I will return to Warner's concepts of a public and participation as well as critiques and developments of these concepts in chapter 2. Suffice it to say for the present that by reworking the groups of citizen journalistic expressions in firmer relation to the emergence of a public, citizen journalism may be conceived as an act of addressing and bringing into being a particular community – as being situated and grounded in relation to the particular needs, memories and desires of a community. Citizen journalism may also be defined as political – that is, exercising citizen engagement and social belonging in opposition to the mainstream and often with a desire to enable social change (Blaagaard 2013). Finally, citizen journalism may be understood as embodiment and speaking from a certain historical, social, geographic and economic standpoint, marked by race, gender, religion, class, sexuality and 'diffabilities'. The three modes of engagement (situated, political and embodied modalities) are the points from which this book's analysis establishes a perspective of citizen journalism as conceptual practice. They are the grounded points in citizen journalism's politics of location, and as such they are unashamedly poststructuralist.

Chapter 1

DELEUZE ON CONCEPTUAL PERSONAE AND PRACTICE: A POLITICS OF LOCATION

The concept of citizen journalism as a situated, political and embodied practice adopts an approach inspired by the 'politics of location' favoured by feminist Deleuzian philosopher Rosi Braidotti (2011), the activist and poetic work of Adrienne Rich (1984) and the thinking of Deleuze and Guattari (1994). Viewing citizen journalism as conceptual practice is a cartographic strategy for grounding activism by activating a set of counter-memories and counter-readings or ways of thinking against the grain of dominant social representations (Braidotti 2011, 271). Reading *The Herald* as citizen journalistic conceptual practice brings about a grounded cartography that shifts perspective and shows citizen journalism to be an embodied political act: Rather than focussing on citizen journalism's structural implications relative to established 'truths', it uses the case – or 'immanent plane', in Deleuzian terms – to discover the embedded events and politics inherent in *The Herald*'s citizen journalism.

What Braidotti calls materialist and vital, embedded and embodied thought, or 'politics of location' (Braidotti 2011, 2013a) resonates with Deleuze and Guattari's *conceptual personae* and more broadly 'conceptual practice', which is their way of demystifying the transcendental power of concepts and grounding them in situated and embodied thought. For Deleuze and Guattari (1994, 20–21), a concept is a processual act of thought. A concept is defined by the variations within and amongst its components and qualities, so that the concept of a journalism may be defined by its particular practices, implications and relations rather than by its general terminology and universalist assumptions. These defining practices, implications and relations are not constant but are determined through planes of immanence – empirical cases of theoretical relevance – and their inter-relatedness. Deleuze and Guattari argue that spaces or planes of immanence are marked by movements of territorialization, deterritorialization and reterritorialization – that is, movements in the locations of political power. Movements of territorialization are antithetical to a nationalistic focus and to the traditional idea of modern journalism's social and political role due to their processes of continuous uprooting and re-rooting, which dissuade teleological thinking and methodological nationalism. 'Social fields', according to Deleuze and Guattari (1994, 68, italics in original), 'are inextricable knots in which the three movements [of territorialization, deterritorialization and reterritorialization] are mixed up so that, in order to disentangle them, we have to *diagnose real types or personae*'. In Braidotti's work, this becomes an emphasis on 'figurations' – that is, visualisations and imaginary constructions which function as navigational tools to enable us to think through the ever-shifting conditions of the real world. Looking at citizen journalism in this light permits an analytical approach that neither praises citizen journalism for its unique and new presentations of possibilities nor neglects its political potential but instead insists upon a grounded analysis of situated and embodied politics of cultural and social change.

The conceptual thinking of Deleuze and Guattari as well as Braidotti rejects abstract generalisations and insists on the concept's limited knowledge of itself, 'not to be confused with the state of affairs in which it is embodied' (Deleuze and Guattari 1994, 33). While it may be limited in terms of what it can tell us about citizen journalism as a generalised idea, the conceptual personae or figurations favoured by Deleuze and Guattari and Braidotti allow for new perspectives on what citizen journalism may entail and may be able to procure in terms of political subjectivity, grounded activism and social change. To iterate the points made above: This book does not define citizen journalism but instead explores what citizen journalism can do and what meaning-making processes follow from it. I prefer to use the term 'conceptual practice' introduced by Deleuze (1989) in *Cinema 2* rather than 'conceptual personae', which I understand as part of the former. Conceptual practice is the process of philosophy in which an artistic or professional social practice or grounded event (such as cinema or citizen journalism) is used to extract concepts or events in order to rethink and reformulate their potential and relations in the community or field (280). Philosophy itself is the creative practice of conceptualising, rather than being abstract theory, 'pre-existent, ready-made in a prefabricated sky' (280).

If philosophy is a practical job, planes of immanence, conceptual personae, and reterritorialization and deterritorialization are tools of the trade. The conceptual persona is the figuration which allows a counter-reading of the field by drawing a different map and image than do mainstream social representations, whereas the planes of immanence are the spaces that 'secure conceptual linkages with ever increasing connections' (Deleuze and Guattari 1994, 37). The plane of immanence is the 'indivisible milieu' (36) that the concepts populate, the glue and coherence of the concepts. 'Thinking', Deleuze and Guattari (88) assert, 'consists in stretching out a plane of immanence that absorbs the earth (or rather "adsorbs" it)'. Like Rich's metaphorical earth from which theory and concepts may be extracted and returned to fertilise our understanding, Deleuze and Guattari speak of the plane of immanence as an earth on which concepts arise and waves of territorializations, deterritorializations and reterritorializations roll. Thinking, then, is not a teleological act that depends upon origin, necessity or history but instead a continuous movement that breathes through contingency and becoming. In these movements, memory and the collective recollection of nationhood and citizenship gain importance. This is because 'the deep generative powers of memory [are understood] as a political project' (Braidotti 2006a, 167). The generative powers of memory are active remembrance – that which returns and is remembered or repeated (168) – which support and sustain a 'becoming-minoritarian'. Following Deleuze and Guattari (2004 [1980]), Braidotti presents her complex thinking of ethical relations through the concept of becoming-minoritarian, which in this sense is a collective process of deterritorializing the subject and opening up spaces for reinvention of a self.

In order to think about citizen journalism as conceptual practice, we must engage the modes of concepts, planes of immanence, personae, deterritorializations and reterritorializations or think of citizen journalism as an event or gesture, one that may be continuously repeated with a difference, which determines the change to which it may contribute. Paul Patton (2006) discusses Deleuze's use of the concept of the event in relation to the legal dimensions of colonisation. Events, Patton tells us, stand in relation to language in that they are incorporeal transformations brought about through illocutionary speech acts (Austin 1962). Understood in this way, language is more than just representation but entails a 'primary function . . . to act upon the world' (Patton 2006, 111). Second, events 'are not universals, but singular incorporeal entities' and are also recurrent (112), meaning that the event is repeatable in different settings, times and spaces. The event may recur in different elements, while remaining an expression of the same event. Furthermore, the event draws upon a different concept of time that is co-extensive with 'becomings' and that is defined by the transformation involved. Patton (118) uses the example of water at zero degrees Celsius, when water is freezing or ice is thawing, depending on whether the temperature is in the process of increasing or decreasing. The event, then, is a complex relation which requires an external perspective to be properly realised. It may also be understood as a way of counter-reading historical circumstances so as to avoid charges of historicism. My claim, then, is that if a colonial newspaper may serve as an example of citizen journalism, we may be able to understand citizen journalism as more than just a product of particular Western concepts of freedom and histories of political subjectivity drawing upon the enlightenment and humanism. Instead, citizen journalism in the colonial setting of St. Croix – conceived of in terms of an event-generating concept of political acts and practices –sheds light on the possibilities and the limitations of these concepts without reducing them to their histories or origins.

The Deleuzian modes and concepts described above will help us undertake a cartography, to situate an ever-moving image or event of what citizen journalism can do and to explore its political and social implications. For example, we may be able to explore what citizen journalism does to the idea of the citizen as well as what kind of public or community citizen journalism may produce. In order to accomplish this, the following reading of *The Herald* and understanding of citizen journalism will explore not just the practices of Jackson and the newspaper he published but also the colonial setting – as portrayed in the newspaper and as cultural historical fact – in which these practices took place and their relations to the colonizer, the potentially cosmopolitan relationship to the community of African American culture in New York and to the progressive politics of early twentieth-century Copenhagen. These relations may be seen as movements of deterritorialization, whereas the journalistic ritual of the newspaper, especially after 1917, may call upon the concept of reterritorialization. The particular conditions of the practice of citizen journalism allow for a grounded theorisation of what citizen journalism entails and enables. It is also these particular and historical circumstances that invite a postcolonial reading. The situated, political and embodied implications of *The Herald* are of a particular nature, grounded in African diaspora and displacement, the civil rights movement, socialism and the racial politics of the United States as well as the Danish colonies, which carried – and continue to carry – harsh corporeal, embodied memories and consequences. I suggest in chapters 4 and 5 that *The Herald* represents an expressive vernacular culture as theorised by postcolonial thinker Paul Gilroy (1994). Subjectivity formations brought about by citizen journalistic practices, then, are on the one hand understood in terms of content circulating and addressing a public and on the other hand seen in the repetitions of particular formats or expressions, such as certain events and gestures.

SPIVAK AND ONWARDS: POSTCOLONIAL REFLECTIONS

When combining Deleuze with postcolonial reality and theory, it is necessary to acknowledge that the Deleuzian theories have not always been well received in studies of postcolonial situations and relations. Gayatri Spivak (1988) introduced a critical reading of Deleuze's and Michel Foucault's work in her piece 'Can the Subaltern Speak?', in which she argues that the two poststructuralist philosophers are guilty of re-inaugurating a transparent European subject despite claiming to dismantle this subject. Taking her starting point in a published conversation between Deleuze and Foucault, Spivak (272) critiques their thinking, in which, she states, they 'systematically ignore the question of ideology and their own implication in intellectual and economic history', thereby rendering invisible their complicity in upholding Western philosophical hegemony. If the subject of power is transparent, it follows that Deleuze and Foucault leave it up to the subaltern to simply speak on equal terms. But, Spivak argues, this is in fact impossible for subaltern subjects: There is no voice outside Western discourse, and ignoring this fact is a failing and is incompatible with postcolonial thinking and critique. Deleuze and Foucault are moreover blamed for showing a lack of interest in the actual and authentic lives of minorities and postcolonial struggles; they instead employ abstract concepts such as becoming-minoritarian and nomadic. On occasion, these concepts are 'perceived to contribute to the demolition of consistent expressions of selfhood' needed to engage in common strategies of resistance (Bignall and Patton 2010, 2). However, concepts of resistance in binary opposition to hegemonic thought and power are not part of Deleuzian thinking, given that Deleuze theorises a 'third alternative', in which he 'posits against the lacking divided self [the subaltern], not an un-divided self, but a non-lacking divided self' (Robinson and Tormey 2010, 35). Deleuze's concepts of becoming and nomadism are affirmative alternatives to the philosophies of lack and negativity, which, Robinson and Tormey strongly assert, are as much inheritors of European and colonial thought as are the philosophies of affirmation that Spivak chastises for making their European roots invisible. As for Foucault, inherent in his thought is an antihumanist critique of Western claims to universalism. Spivak (1988, 291–94), however, hails Jacques Derrida alone for not generalising European history and economy but instead for positioning Europe as one amongst many possible narratives, despite the fact that both Foucault and Deleuze could be said to unhesitatingly challenge these narratives as well. In their detailed and comprehensive reproach to the argument forwarded by Spivak, Andrew Robinson and Simon Tormey (2010) list five points of Spivak's critique, which they firmly refute one by one, often by pointing to thorough readings of the body of work of Deleuze, which they claim Spivak fails to consider. However, Spivak's essay does not simply criticise Deleuze and Foucault but also offers a pivotal reading of the position of the formerly colonised or subaltern peoples in discourse. As Bignall and Patton (2010, 5) put it in their introduction to one of the few collections of engagements between Deleuze and postcolonial theory, if the resistance to colonialism is only heard through particular discourses or formats, then limits are simultaneously imposed on the content, on what may be expressed. It follows that if the formerly colonised subject is to be able to speak for herself, what is required are alternative forms of listening. Interestingly, it is precisely in forms of listening or 'speaking before' that Robinson and Tormey (31–32) find similarities in the projects of Spivak and Deleuze. Spivak's project is to practice an aspiration and desire for unlearning privilege in order to attempt to place oneself in the position of the other. This movement, Robinson and Tormey (31) argue, is very close to the Deleuzian never-ending process of becoming-minoritarian, which 'introduce[es] otherness and creat[es] new flows'. Becoming-minoritarian is seen as a productive, affirmative and qualitative engagement with the other, which Robinson and Tormey moreover liken to the pedagogy of Paulo Freire (1996), seemingly despite the latter's Marxist approach. Freire positions a dialogical pedagogy of problem-posing education as opposed to a teacher-regulated narrative of what he calls banking-education. Whereas banking-education presupposes that students are ignorant and empty vessels to be filled with knowledge (as in a repository), problem-posing education relies upon dialogue and the shared knowledge production between student and teacher. It is fair to say that, as a fellow Marxist, Freire is situated squarely within Spivak's social structure of hegemonic system versus counter-hegemonic resistance. Nevertheless, Freire's concept of praxis, which entails both grounded activism and reflection, and which is based on dialogue between the oppressor and the oppressed (or teacher and student), may be a common denominator, since both Spivak and Deleuze presuppose a recognition of difference and, importantly, of asymmetry. In this manner, Freire (1996) moreover disputes the notion of absolute truth or knowledge – that is, universalism. The resonances between the two traditions are not lost on Braidotti. While identifying with the theories of post-humanism, Braidotti (2013a, 18) writes: 'Western post-humanism on the one hand and non-Western neo-humanism on the other transpose hybridity, nomadism, diasporas, creolization processes into means of re-grounding claims to connections and alliances among different constituencies'. In other words, postcolonialism and poststructuralism are not only compatible; they work within similar rhythms and modalities to bring attention to a plethora of diverse subjectivity formations.

Arguably, *The Herald* is an example of the particular setting and format through which subaltern, colonised subjects are able to express themselves: through the Westernised format of individual freedom of speech and print and through the ideal of journalism's objectivity and rationality. However, the analyses and conclusions reached in chapters 3, 4 and 5 of this book also question this format's stability and reliability, asking whether these tenets of Western freedom – speech and identity – as expressed in citizen journalism can be understood as a development stemming from the particular, embodied experiences of colonised subjects rather than from the white, privileged universal man of Western thought. If so, citizen journalism may be seen as an embodied, political and public dialogue in a social field of multiple differences in which grounded activism – paired with reflection, counter-readings and counter-memories – becomes a means of thinking against the grain of dominant social representations (Braidotti 2011, 271).

BRAIDOTTI ON THE DETERRITORIALIZATION OF IDENTITY

In her essay on 'The Becoming-Minoritarian of Europe', Rosi Braidotti (2006b) presents an interesting response to or extension of Robinson and Tormey's Deleuzian reproach to Spivak's negative (both in terms of criticism and in terms of philosophy) reading of Foucault and Deleuze. If Robinson and Tormey (2010) stop short of presenting a Deleuzian non-universalist engagement with a postcolonial situation, Braidotti calls for a deterritorialization of European whiteness and of identity in a move which she, using a Deleuzian term, calls a process of becoming-minoritarian. Robinson and Tormey call becoming-minoritarian an affirmative and qualitative engagement with the other, and Braidotti adds specificity. First, Braidotti presents the crux of the European situation in terms that much resemble the critique levelled at European subjects by Spivak: The myth of European cultural and religious homogeneity naturalises whiteness, making it invisible and all-consuming, and 'the prerogative of being dominant is that a concept defined oppositionally produces the marks of oppression and/or marginalisation' (Braidotti 2006b, 82). Second, what is needed to deterritorialize whiteness is a view from another – marginalised – perspective, an understanding of the self that transcends the pain and melancholy of losing the self. Referring to the work of Glissant, Braidotti (84) advances a 'sense of openness' and rhizomatic thinking akin to the Freirean dialogue discussed above as well as Gilroy's concept of 'the Black Atlantic' (Gilroy 1994), which will be discussed in chapter 4. The hybrid or middle is a privileged position for shifting our thinking, Braidotti (2006b, 85) argues, following Glissant, but '[t]he point is not merely to deconstruct identities or loudly proclaim counter-identities but to open up identity to different connections able to produce multiple belongings that in turn precipitate a non-unitary vision of a subject'. This insistence on multiplicity is clearly in line with Deleuze's non-lacking divided self, discussed above and carried over to the third point: Braidotti goes on to argue for what she calls a double necessity of accountability for history and white oppression of others as well as a deterritorialization, which is a conscious shifting of perspectives and identifications, a rooted movement allowed to flow. This move, echoed by Robinson and Tormey, bypasses Spivak's critique of Deleuze and Foucault, which is based on a binary position between the unitary and universal European subject and the lacking, Lacanian subject of the formerly colonised. Rather than accepting the binary pair and arguing for a change of perspective from a majoritarian (or a politically and culturally powerful) position to a position identifying with minorities or racialized subjects, Braidotti (91) calls for a becoming-minoritarian: a qualitative – affirmative and creative – shift 'akin to shedding old skin'. Becoming-minoritarian entails rejecting the zero-sum game of binary thinking and realising a multidirectional analysis (Rothberg 2009) of politics of location. Affirmative thinking and creativity involves generating new memories and narratives (Braidotti 2013b), imagining or remembering ourselves as who we are (Braidotti 2006a, 168). Again, Braidotti's Deleuzian philosophy finds perhaps a surprising bedfellow in postcolonial thinking: Paul Gilroy is a much-cited postcolonial and antiracist thinker who identifies the process of melancholia as a means of dealing with the postcolonial reality of European states, theorised through the lens of the United Kingdom's colonial past as well as the United States' cultural products and expressions. Gilroy (2004, 4) suggests 'that multicultural ethics and politics could be premised upon an agonistic, planetary humanism capable of comprehending the universality of our elemental vulnerability to the wrongs we visit upon each other'. Unacknowledged racial hierarchies are what keep societies from realising this convivial cosmopolitanism. Gilroy (12–13) therefore, like Braidotti, urges new imaginaries that break down the norm of national identities based on nostalgic reminiscing about a whitewashed past and drive us to remember how these narratives and memories came about, when and how they entered the human sciences and corrupted government, justice and communication. Unlike Braidotti, however, Gilroy reimagines the human as the centre of these narratives. While Gilroy and Braidotti agree on the necessity of thinking and remembering differently in order to bring about a political activism based on critical theoretical engagements, their conceptualisations of the human differ. Gilroy insists on revisiting the modern racial hierarchies of humanity – not to dwell on the atrocities or to highlight the grandeur of empire but to critically assess and understand the enduring and powerful impact these hierarchies had and to undo them and establish new relationships. The poststructuralist, antihumanist critique is rescinded by Gilroy in favour of a deconstruction of racial hierarchies that made the white, European male the measure of humanity. Gilroy believes that producing a counter-historical narrative can help redefine liberal modernity and present us with the potential for a planetary humanism. In contrast, Braidotti escapes both melancholia and nostalgia by insisting on affirmative becomings. The concept of the human is no longer at the centre of subjectivity, yet the questions of who counts as human and who can appear to others remain crucial. The possibilities for creating new affirmative subject formations weaken the power of exclusion from the public.

FROM THE PERSPECTIVE OF THIS BOOK

For Braidotti, memory is akin to imagination and creative production of possible futures and new relations. This is why Braidotti takes a post-human position that focusses on the continued production of subjectivities and intensities of relations, rather than the categories of the modern human. Chapter 4's analysis of *The Herald*'s relationship to memory and history draws upon both Gilroy's and Braidotti's conceptualisations of memory's productive power. Chapter 5 brings their work into today's realm of visuality and aesthetic citizen journalism as political acts. The ongoing debate on humanism and universalism is dealt with in chapters 2 and 3. Whereas the political content of *The Herald* relates to humanism akin to what may be termed 'new humanism', in which deconstruction of hierarchies is pivotal and constitutive of further expressions and formations of subjectivity, the theoretical discussion of citizen journalism more broadly encompasses elaborations upon the format of the practice, arguing for citizen journalism as a particular, grounded practice, which does not take the central notion of *the* human – critiqued or universal – as a starting point.

So how does this book combine or situate the (post)colonial critique and geography with the Deleuzian thinking on subjectivity to which it subscribes? The colonial aspects and perspectives in this book are both empirical and methodological. First, the colonial case of *The Herald* provides an empirical setting that permits exploration of a political and social space defined by industrialisation, technology and modernity. The fact that the newspaper was edited and published by a formerly colonised subject brings forth a narrative that obstructs the tale of modernity arriving from Europe and calls into question the sovereignty of citizens and borders of colonial Denmark. This is not to say that the heritage and identity of *The Herald*'s editor, Jackson, determines the newspaper's degree of subversiveness. To the contrary, the construction of national or social community and belonging is complex and ambiguous. *The Herald* constitutes an assemblage of African Caribbean, African American and Danish progressive, socialist political drives for civil rights and equality, sustained only partly independently from the policies of the colonisers. Simultaneously, *The Herald*, as a newspaper and a journalistic product, is very much embedded in the project of modernity. In order to unpack this claim, a discussion of the emergence of the citizen subject (Balibar 1989, Isin 2012) and the colonial uncoupling of jurisdiction and territorial state control (Benhabib 2007, 23) as well as the imbrication of the idea of the state, the people and the nation (Isin 2012) will take place in chapter 2. Second, this independent political emergence of the formerly colonised people of St. Croix through the pages of *The Herald* calls for a methodological shift, a rethinking of the tenets upon which citizen journalism is constructed. How do we think and conceptualise citizen journalism at this event of colonial transition and political becoming? What are the implications of this thinking? In answering these questions, I rely upon the similarities between poststructuralist and postcolonial thinking when it comes to deconstructing universals and historicisms. The perhaps more specific historically grounded political theories of postcolonial thinking provide the backbone of my critical reading and (as it should be clear at this point) I see no conflict – quite the opposite – between these concepts and those of Deleuze, with which I simultaneously engage. In this, as argued above, I follow Braidotti's (2014, 18) emphasis on the 'resonances between their efforts and respective political aims and passions'. My analysis and theorisation hopefully contribute to a project of 'provincializing Europe' in the sense similar to that described by the historian and postcolonial scholar Dipesh Chakrabarty (2000). Like Spivak, Chakrabarty engages with the issue of subaltern representation. Chakrabarty (7–11) recognises this representation as existing within a system featuring the figure of Europe as the sole originator of the nation-state and within the asymmetrical, scholarly obligation to know European history as that which came before and colonial history as the 'not yet'. Importantly, like Braidotti and Deleuze, Chakrabarty (35) underscores a desire to circumvent the narrative of subaltern lack and instead 'read "plenitude" and "creativity" where this narrative has made us read "lack" and "inadequacy."' Although Chakrabarty (166) does not elaborate upon this point immediately, his later work on Deleuze and the concept of repetition through which 'newness enters the world' hints at a different perspective from that of Spivak.

While this introduction focusses on the book's methodological and theoretical implications, the second chapter turns to locating the book's particular conceptual thinking and emphasis on the political act. The critique of modern journalistic ideologies supported by Deleuzian and postcolonial thinking has implications for the conceptualisation of the citizen relative to the wider scholarly field of citizen journalism. While citizen journalism as a scholarly field has been developed in terms of focus on the concept of the citizen, chapter 2 discusses the ways in which this concept takes on new political agency from a Deleuzian perspective. The chapter develops an argument for a perspective on the political potential of citizen journalism that circumvents the traditional Habermasian public sphere as a point of departure. Poststructuralism's dispute with humanism is then exemplified by the dispute between Habermas's humanist concept of the public sphere and the subjectivity formation of citizen journalism's multiple publics and citizen subjects. By engaging in a counter-reading of *The Herald*, citizen journalism is theorised as a series of political acts in their own right and on their own terms. Chapter 2 hereby operationalizes the methodological concepts presented in this first chapter, at the same time as it elaborates and expands upon the preceding discussions of conceptual personae and politics of location to discuss theories of citizenship and subjectivity. The chapter further builds the case for an analytical perspective that 'express[es] complex singularities, not universal claims' (Braidotti 2013a, 164; 2011). The meaning of 'political act' will be presented and discussed in line with the work of Isin (2002) and Isin and Nielsen (2008) as well as the work of other theorists spanning the disciplines of anthropology, social sciences, political theory, and media and globalisation studies. The concept of 'cosmopolitanism' is used to consider the global reach and intermingled cultures present in citizen journalism, such as that which Jackson created in *The Herald*.

Chapter 3 follows up on this by undertaking a cartography of the counter-position of citizen journalism and links it to the theories of citizenship in *The Herald*. It engages in a closer reading of *The Herald*'s coverage of the issue of American citizenship, analysed through a multidirectional reading of the content of *The Herald*. The Virgin Islands were sold by Denmark to the United States in 1916 and transferred to US jurisdiction in 1917, where they remain today as an unincorporated territory. Contrary to islanders' expectations, the islands' political subjects were not granted US citizenship until ten years later, in 1927. Published between 1915 and 1925, *The Herald* thus provides us with a unique opportunity to analyse concrete ways in which citizen journalism functions as a political act, enabling citizen practices. If political acts are understood as acts that 'disrupt' and create 'rupture in the given' (Isin and Nielsen 2008, 10, 25) and are understood in opposition to institutionalised citizenship practices, as I argue in chapter 2, then how does citizen journalism in *The Herald* negotiate and navigate the terms of the political at a time and in a space of civic and institutional tension? Chapters 4 and 5 answer this question, and the analyses map ways in which *The Herald*'s citizen journalism territorializes, deterritorializes and reterritorializes citizenship debates through its address to the African Caribbean public. In this manner, the book sheds light on how the counterpublic produced through citizen journalistic political acts may coexist with the institutional policy-driven discourses within *The Herald*. This book's analytical chapters put to the test this conceptual approach to citizen journalism.

Shifting perspectives on citizen journalism in order to understand the practice and the act as a politics of location requires a continuous revisiting of three questions: First, who counts as human – that is, who is able to appear on his or her own terms? This is not a question of access alone but rather a question of political subjectivity rooted in a critique of modernity. Second, how can citizen journalism be conceptualised as a political act that forges a space of appearance and potential subjectivity formation? And third, if citizen journalism acts on the world – visually and linguistically – by forging such a space, to what extent does this alter public spaces and concepts of citizenship and civil rights? Moreover, the relationship between space (in terms of colonial possessions and positions, national boundaries and cosmopolitan connections) and time (in terms of memory, counter-memory, historicity and the future) represents an axis on which shifting answers to the above questions turn. This book, then, sets forth the genealogy and creativity of a politics of locations in *The Herald*, which becomes a figuration of citizen journalistic act and practice. In so doing, it draws upon poststructuralist and postcolonial theory and thereby invites a new perspective on citizen journalism.

NOTE

1. In chapter 2, I explore the assertion that this narrative could be seen as an outcome of the humanist traditions of journalism studies, which place great value on rationality and consensus reasoning.

2

Deconstructing the Citizen Journalist

Benedict Anderson (1991, 44–45) defines the relationship between capitalism and print languages as foundational for national consciousness, with the press playing a particularly significant role in creating and supporting national identity. Anderson sees this relationship as important in three ways: First, the relationship created a common field of communication and commerce. Second, print capitalism's – in Anderson's terminology – permanent form and the possibility of reprinting gave a new fixity to the language. Third, print capitalism allowed some languages to become national dialects and others to become less meaningful, thereby creating a hierarchy of expression. In terms of establishing a common 'we', early newspapers such as *The Herald* assembled seemingly eclectic events into a whole, defined by the commonality of readership. This was especially important in the colonies. 'What was brought together, on the same page, *this* marriage with *this* ship, *this* price with *that* bishop, was the very structure of the colonial administration and market-system itself' (62), with the result that national identity seemed to stretch across geographically remote and detached areas.

The Danish colonies of St. Croix, St. Thomas and St. John, however, were multilingual, with a preference for English rather than Danish. Although Danish was the official language under the Danish flag, English was the language of the press. *The Herald* was published in English, with the exceptions of official notifications, which were published in Danish as well as in English translation. The editor of *The Herald*, David Hamilton Jackson, knew the Danish language but is only known to have given speeches and written texts in English. Leaving the issue of commerce aside for now, the fact that *The Herald* and the Danish colonies to a large extent lacked a common language challenges the argument that print capitalism is crucial to sustaining a colonial sense of belonging to the nationality of the colonial ruler. As chapters 3 and 4 explore, Jackson often drew attention to his and the islands' identification with Danish politics and culture. But more importantly, *The Herald* and the particularities of the colonies in which it was published and distributed may serve as an example of how print capitalism was employed to work against a fixed national identity formation and instead to emphasise, on the one hand, a cosmopolitan citizenship and, on the other, a claim to civil rights specific to descendants of enslaved labourers.

Another challenge to national fixity in *The Herald* was the fact that Jackson was a descendant of enslaved Africans. In his work on the relationship between race and state formations, David T. Goldberg (2002, 108) argues that race 'is not a premodern condition but a quintessentially modern one masquerading in the guise of the given and the ancient, bloodlines and genetic pools'. Colonial differentiations between 'races' were based on either a notion of naturalism or of historicism: Whereas the former held that racially identified subjects were 'inherently inferior' (106) and therefore unable to qualify for citizenship, the latter was based on the not-yet (see also Chakrabarty, 2000): 'Citizenship was a status and standing not only never quite (to be) reached for the racially immature but for whom the menu of rights was never quite (as) complete' (Goldberg 2002, 106). Goldberg's theorisation is relevant to the case of *The Herald* because of his understanding of the roles of race and colonial state formation in developing the concept of the citizen. Here, Goldberg takes as his starting point that 'the modernist conception of citizenship . . . has built into it as a constitutive condition the *identification* of individual citizen with the state' (266–67; emphasis in original). Goldberg (267) identifies three resultant logics: (1) citizenship is built on ideas of identity, (2) the state is homogenous and coherent and (3) citizens remain immobile and within the boundaries and borders of the state. These modern logics support Anderson's assertion of how the press continuously establishes a common national 'we', which in turn produces a right to citizenship. If citizenship is premised on racial and linguistic markers that are understood to be stable over time, it may also define who is recognised as a speaking subject and therefore a participating subject within a national-colonial public. However, again, *The Herald* seems to both cement and challenge the theories through its call for recognition using the format of the modern newspaper – that is, disrupting the coherent, imaginary nation-state and its supposedly immobile citizens using the tools of the modern master (Lorde 2007 [1978]).

A final challenge, then, lies in the mobility of Jackson and *The Herald*, in terms of both physical and intellectual travels across continents and cultures. While colonial history and geography represent the paradoxical uncoupling of jurisdiction and territory (Benhabib 2007, 26), *The Herald* forges bridges and a global territory, or ecumene (Hannerz, 1996), that may eventually lay the groundwork for an understanding of the development from subjects as *subjectus* – or subjects to power (Isin and Ruppert 2015, 22) – to citizen subjects as understood by Etienne Balibar (1989). 'Europe's colonies', Seyla Benhabib (23, emphasis in original) asserts, 'become the site of usurpation and conquest in which *extra-juridical spaces*, removed from the purview of liberal principles of consent, are created'. *The Herald* continuously called out the limits to the liberal principles of civil rights and freedoms, yet as chapters 4 and 5 show, Jackson was not always successful in these endeavours.

The three challenges of language, race and territory allow us to think critically about journalism's role in the process of becoming a citizen. The relationships between race, state and citizenship are relevant to the discussion of citizen journalism because of its theorisation and conceptualisation of the citizen. Many studies on mediated citizenship, I argue, rely on an unspoken, modern conceptualisation and understanding of what it means to be a citizen and on how one becomes a citizen. However, this chapter shows how different ideas of participation and public engagement present different concepts of the citizen, and I argue that citizen journalism requires an actively acting citizen – a becoming-citizen.

Following Foucault, Goldberg explains the process of governance as fundamental to the colonial, racial state. The embodiment and reiteration of the everyday by the colonial subject as well as the simultaneous production and maintenance of the colonial state project lead him to think of the racial state as a *political force* in which subjects and institutions take part (Goldberg 2002, 108–9). This is a conceptualisation of the relationship between state and citizen that posits the (im)possibility of subjects engaging politically and being recognised within the national public. The case of *The Herald* illustrates the construction of citizenship's fickleness and calls for a more careful theorisation of citizen journalism as political acts rather than as a technological opportunity or challenge to professional journalism, as described in chapter 1.

In order to analyse the intricate relationship between the role of the press, the national public and the citizen, in the section 'The Participating and Performing Citizen', I begin by presenting media theories on becoming and enacting citizenship through media. This discussion is far from exhaustive but instead sketches issues of participation (so broadly conceptualised by Warner [2002]) and performativity (often referred to via Austin [1962] and Butler [1993]) in citizen and media studies, and in this chapter explored through the influential work of Lilie Chouliaraki. These practices of participation and performativity, I argue, allow for political engagement within a participatory public modelled after, but not identical to, the Habermasian public sphere. The participatory public is underscored by theoretical and empirical studies on digitally mediated participation. The section elaborates upon the different modalities in which journalism may produce, sustain, challenge and disrupt the concept of the public within which an acting citizen is assumed.

In the section 'The Citizen, the Subject, the Press', I shift perspectives in order to advance an oppositional conceptualisation of how citizens may engage with and disrupt public formations. Leaning on the thinking of Engin Isin and Etienne Balibar, I argue that the citizen of citizen journalism must be political, not despite but because of her position outside the established public. A citizen is created through oppositional acts. Following this conceptualisation of the citizen subject, based on readings of Balibar, Isin and others, I further explore the possibilities of a form of cosmopolitan practice in colonies that questions the stability and coherence of the nation-state. In the section 'Colonialism, Cosmopolitanism and Deterritorializations', I pursue this through readings of Ulf Hannerz's (1996, 22) transnational connections and 'global habitats of meaning', Benhabib's (2007, 31; 2006) concept of 'democratic iterations', and Terhi Rantanen's (2007) idea of cosmopolitanization of news. While Hannerz and Rantanen belong to an anthropological and cultural studies tradition, I also wish to draw upon the politico-legal understanding of the citizen provided by Benhabib, while remaining aligned with Foucault, Balibar and Isin on the issues of subjectivity and governmentality.

Straddling these diverse traditions and bringing them together through my reading of *The Herald* is necessary for exploring the diverse paths that run through the field. I strive to keep the idea of the political in play so as to avoid reducing colonial acts of resistance and political participation to either cultural and social interactions or to legal institutions alone. I instead insist on conceptualising the political as a process of affirmative subjectivity formation. Following the trajectory outlined above, I seek to ground the discussion in a particular political, colonial setting and in terms of particular possibilities for acting in order to argue for how Jackson's colonial newspaper *The Herald* may be regarded as *citizen* journalism. It is *citizen* journalism not because it allowed participation or created a coherent population but because it entailed a political act in a profoundly dispersed colonial setting and by an editor who held a precarious and ambiguous status as a not-yet citizen in politico-legal terms.

This outline has already diverged significantly from most conceptualisations of the citizen in citizen journalism coming out of media and journalism studies. With the notable exception of Isin and Ruppert (2015), it is rare to find theorisations about the relationship between citizenship and citizen journalism in the literature (Allan 2013, 16). Moreover, it is difficult to find arguments against the modern foundations of journalism and their connections with nation-state formations. Writings on journalism's role in portraying citizens (e.g., Lewis, Inthorn and Wahl-Jørgensen, 2007) and in constructing citizenship (e.g., Dahlgren, 2009) belong to a growing literature, yet despite the prolific writings on citizen journalism (Wall 2015, Allan 2013, Allan and Thorsen 2009) and social media (van Dijck 2013, Fuchs 2014, Rettberg 2014), inquiries into what kind of citizenship is constructed through the practice of citizen journalism are few and far between. In the following, I thus address this gap in the literature by discussing how the citizen has been conceptualised as participating, countered, voicing, performing and digitalising her citizenship through media.

THE PARTICIPATING AND PERFORMING CITIZEN

It is common to begin discussions of journalism and citizenship with a reference to Jürgen Habermas, whose 1962 book *Strukturwandel der Öffentlichkeit* was translated into English in 1989. Indeed, the publication has already been duly mentioned in the previous chapter of this book. Habermas's book is important because it presents mass media, the institution of journalism, as a potential site for public address and deliberation. Through mass media, the bourgeois public may engage in debate and enact their discursive citizenship. For this reason, the public sphere has received significant attention from media scholars over the years (Lunt and Livingstone 2013). Because it is through mass media and media more generally that citizens are understood to participate in democracy on an everyday level, this practice of participation has become important in journalism studies' conceptualisation of the citizen. A citizen is someone who participates in a media-defined public, likely through letters to the editor or, more recently, via Twitter, but also in more creative ways, such as photoshopped images and memes through which she engages in and helps sustain a public. Media scholars have, moreover, argued that media is a tool for training democratic thinking (Hartley 2012, Jenkins 1992, 2006) in at least two ways. First, Henry Jenkins (2006) argues that media users have always participated in and made use of media to engage in communities of common interest or to develop and improve storylines of favourite television shows. In this way, fans develop off-screen communities connected to what they are shown on screen. Users are producing a convergence between television and print. With digital media, and particularly with the emergence of Web 2.0, cross-fertilisation between different media platforms has gained popularity and enabled viewers to secure a voice for themselves in a wider realm of interactions. For Jenkins (1992, 2006), then, digital technology presents an opportunity to create more interactions by engaging a wider public and through easier access to freedom of speech, thereby creating opportunities for democratic interaction and productions of publics.

Media users also participate in the creation of new products to an extent that has justified recent literature calling them 'produsers' (e.g., Bruns 2008, Jenkins 1992, 2006), deliberately spelled with an *s* to connote the amalgamation of 'producer' and 'user'. Examples of these products include photoshopped digital visuals that make a political point and fan fiction that reimagines the narrative of TV programmes to fit an identity-political outlook. These accounts are more than enough to justify participation and engagement in a public, following Warner (2002), whose concept of a public simply requires attention from the consumers and users. However, the link between participation and citizenship seems underexplored, and in this argument for participation, an uncomplicated connection between creative participation, commercialisation and political agency remains implicit.

Second, another way of theorising popular media culture as generative of a participatory public is to argue more explicitly that democratic engagements may be modelled on the participatory culture online. Dismissing most citizen theory as operating with the concept of citizenship as 'a static and definable condition', John Hartley (2012, 10) develops the idea of 'media citizenship', 'based on the *use* of popular media by lay audiences for identity-formation, associative relations, and even for periodic actions that reverse "consumer demand" from a corporate strategy to a popular movement' (Hartley 2012, 15; emphasis in original). Like Jenkins, Hartley believes that people may use or overcome neoliberal marketisation of interrelations online through their cultural interactions, interventions and creative modes. Neither Jenkins nor Hartley are blind to the consumerist influences of crowdsourcing or Do-It-Yourself produsing. Nevertheless, their focus is on the interventions in, for example, election campaign communication, such as photoshopped and edited images of candidates that ironize and poke fun to make a political point. But interventions may also utilise the strategies of online gaming or TV game shows that arguably foster democratic tendencies through voting for or against game show participants (van Zoonen 2005).

Although engaging and provocative, this surely is not the kind of participation and deliberation Habermas had in mind for his public sphere. In more recent writings, for example, Habermas (2009, 134) indeed argues that the public sphere – the space of political communication and deliberation – is dependent upon a strong and, if necessary, state-subsidised 'quality press'. Consumers, Habermas asserts, will want entertainment and distraction, but in order for democracy to endure, consumers need to be citizens – that is, endowed with information and education through the press. In the current climate, the press is under pressure from market forces to engage in ever-more frivolous publications in order to please its readership and turn a profit. However, Habermas argues, this development results in a democratic deficit, disabling the public sphere as a space of deliberation. The role of the press in the public sphere is precisely to negotiate through information and education between the institutionalised discourses of the state and informal everyday conversations (135): If the press is unable to frame deliberation and thus turn everyday conversation into political issues by use of argumentation and research, the discursive vitality of the public sphere will be untenable. To avoid this, Habermas suggests that the state subsidise the quality press. The irony of politically regulating the market of the press by subsidising 'the leading media' is not lost on Habermas (137), who notes, with a nod to Adorno's critique of the culture industry, that '[t]he market first provided the stage on which subversive ideas could emancipate themselves from state repression. Yet the market can play this role only as long as economic constraints do not permeate the cultural and political contents disseminated via the market'. Liberties may be put to the service of commercialised powers that in turn restrain the mobility of thought and political manoeuvring. Who is to decide and how when the economic constraints permeate the content of the press to such a degree that it warrants subsidies and control? And are economic constraints always regulatory of content? Clearly, Habermas has little faith in the democratic pedagogy of online gaming or fan communities. But more importantly, he seems to neglect the importance of non-mainstream news outlets in relation to understanding and sustaining a common identity or vision of a public. For instance, while Hartley and Jenkins are largely preoccupied with media and cultural citizenship, Liesbeth van Zoonen (2005, 9) argues that what is at stake is instead 'whether there are articulations of entertainment and politics that are beneficial to citizenship'. In contrast to Habermas, she believes that the critique that popular culture has received in academia as well as in the media – in which popular culture is denounced as a distraction from politics – is problematic and reductive. Van Zoonen resists the critique and insists on focussing on political citizenship and the democratic project expressed in cultural media products. Her efforts lead her to a conclusion that resembles those of Jenkins and Hartley: '[T]he way fans are positioned, the activities they undertake, and the relation they have with their objects are not fundamentally different from what is expected from good citizens in modernist discourse of politics. And thus it would not have to be a problem if politics were more like popular culture' (145).

While the theories of Jenkins, Hartley and van Zoonen conceive of political discursive space as a playful and creative space that seduces the citizen into thinking politically, the public sphere is based on education, consensus and rational argumentation through mainstream news outlets. Here, we may recall chapter 1's mention of Freire's ideas of banking versus problem-posing education and ask whether Habermas might be ignoring the potential for oppression within a state-controlled press. Indeed, subsidised news outlets are only preferable if the systems backing the subsidies are as reliable and conscientious as the journalistic standards the quality press dictates. Even then, Habermas's (2009, 135) idea of the public sphere as based on the fact that 'deliberate conflicts support the supposition that the democratic procedure will lead to more or less reasonable results in the long run' because it encompasses a rational check-list to avoid 'false assertions' and 'value judgments' seems strangely at odds with the creativity and engagement of which publics are also comprised. For Habermas, public participation remains digested and regulated by the educated/ing classes, the press and in some cases perhaps even the state. Despite the fact that Habermas (2009, 134) views public participation in opposition to the 'populist tendencies' of television and the free market, he restricts expressions of the public to the formats already presented by institutions, thereby limiting their creativity and voice.

Notwithstanding Habermas's reluctance regarding entertainment, both his approach and those of Jenkins and others work within a similar modern, participatory public. They do so because they all to some extent rely upon the assumption that all voices may be heard if they are vocalised – through quality news broadcasts or photoshopped memes alike. The participatory public and the Habermasian public sphere are built upon similar modern assumptions of deliberation through participation. While the participatory public and the public sphere accommodate conflictual views and perspectives, this is only possible insofar as they are recognised by other participants as valuable and worthy of discussion. The participatory public is not oppressive, and it is possible to change society and act politically within and through it. The participatory public nevertheless operates in accordance with a particular set of references, which are recognised as valuable in advance, and this makes it difficult to express an opinion from outside or in a different format than that of the already-decided-upon range of relatability. That is, it follows the logic of a citizen of common identity and within a stable public, the boundaries of which are incontestable – a logic of language, race and territory.

Countering the Participatory Public

Creativity and affect are not the only things Habermas is critiqued for overlooking. Nancy Fraser (1990) dismantles Habermas's concept of the public sphere by arguing that it mistakenly builds upon assumptions that undermine its usefulness. Despite Habermas's later revisions of the concept, this critique still goes to the core of why the public sphere is untenable in a realistic mediated world. Fraser's critique bears repeating here: First, she identifies the problem that the concept of the public sphere brackets off individuals' diverse statuses and ranks in society in order to deliver an arena of equal deliberation. This pretence that equality exists is obviously not the same as a transcending of inequality. There can be no equality without diversity. Second, Fraser (67) points to interpublic relations – that is, 'parallel discursive arenas where members of subordinated social groups invent and circulate counter-discourses, which in turn permit them to formulate oppositional interpretations of their identities, interests, and needs'. Habermas overlooks these diverse counterpublics, Fraser asserts, which leads him to idealise the bourgeois public sphere. However, these publics are arenas for the formation of social identities and enable 'voice', as Warner (2002), following Fraser, discovers. Third, Fraser states that, in the public sphere, the public is artificially divorced from the private and undesirable sphere, thereby rendering the issues up for public debate always already limited to a set (public) agenda. This makes it difficult to bring new items to the table. Habermas's civic republican view thus dictates that identities and interests are an outcome of deliberation. At the same time, Fraser argues, it assumes that deliberation must already concern an oblique idea of a continuously defined 'common good', thereby rendering it difficult for minority experiences to be encompassed by the common 'we'. Fraser may be seen to occupy a position within radical democratic thinking (Dahlgren 2009, 67) that underscores the rootedness of difference. This position is crucial to the concept and practice of citizen journalism. Finally, Fraser is far from convinced of the necessity of dividing the state from civil society, as Habermas would have it. This, Fraser points out, is an unsustainable division in actual embodied civic engagements because citizens are embodied and experience the world – both private and public – from their particular location.

Fraser's critique of Habermas's original conceptualisation of the public sphere is as famous as its subject – and for good reason. Fraser makes visible not only the myopic vision presented of the public sphere but also its inability to understand the importance of 'voice' and of minority experiences to the formation of publics. Fraser's critique thus underscores the importance of acknowledging cultural and media citizenships, yet it goes beyond the playful mediated citizenship by highlighting the connection between the underdog position of counterpublics and individual voice – that is, she insists on its political character. In other words, Fraser emphasises the problematic relationship between the perceived homogenous public sphere and the minority publics that are relegated to the private sphere from which they have no opportunity to gain public voice. This may be understood more broadly as a critique of the modern state, which is upheld by the press guarding the participatory public. The feminist and postcolonial critique of modernity and the modern subject is thus pertinent to this discussion. The hierarchized categorizations of human subjects in terms of race, gender and sexuality are re-enacted indirectly through the closed and self-generating system of what defines the 'common good' and who is granted access to the public sphere or participatory public. In order to gain critical traction, participation and the participating citizen must thus be understood using the concepts of counterpublics enabling 'voice'.

Voice and Performativity

Voice and the importance of being heard and taken seriously return us to the matter of recognition as human introduced in chapter 1. This is the topic of Nick Couldry's (2010, 1) scathing critique of neoliberalism, which argues that 'treating people as if they lack that capacity [to narrate] *is* to treat them as if they were not human. . . . Voice is one word for that capacity, but having a voice is never enough. I need to know that my voice matters; indeed, the offer of effective voice is crucial to the legitimacy of modern democracies'. Couldry has a lot riding on the concept of voice, the concept of listening to and engaging with others as legitimate narrators, included in the 'we' that defines commonalities and public importance. The individual, embodied voice becomes the focal point, which to some extent differs from the aforementioned focus on participation in that participation strives to build and interact within a community, while voice arguably addresses the liberal rights claim. However, it is necessary to engage with both traditions of republicanism and liberalism in order to address a public, a group of strangers (Benhabib 2007, 20). Following Couldry's lead, Lilie Chouliaraki (2012, 2) introduces the edited volume *Self-Mediations: New Media, Citizenship and Civil Selves* by stating: 'Mediated self-presentation entails a particular view of publicness that thematises performance, voice and claims to recognition'. Alongside Couldry's voice and recognition, Chouliaraki offers two additional concepts, which are deemed important to this kind of citizenship: publicness and performance. Performative publicness, Chouliaraki (2) explains, is based on the individual's narrative in contrast to the collective of Fraser's publics; it encompasses visuals and other aesthetics in its performance; and finally, like participatory publics, performative publicness introduces 'a new emphasis on the affective and playful dimensions of public communication'. Performative publicness potentially fuses participation and voice in a new kind of political arena.

While performative publicness is founded on speech act theory, the details of how this becomes a political subjectivity or citizenship remain vague. Indeed, it is uncertain whether the concept of voice does not, like the public sphere, neglect the different positions and (in)abilities to speak and set the agenda. Arguably, voices may differ, but the format within which they are audible remains the same. Chouliaraki (2013a, 192) herself provides an answer: In the specific realm of humanitarian communication, ethico-political engagements occur in the 'theatrical imagination'. The theatrical imagination – following Hannah Arendt's idea of 'the space of appearance', elaborated upon by Silverstone (2007) – mobilises empathy and challenges judgement in an agonistic space. Agonism, Chouliaraki (193) argues, grounds empathetic imagination in 'the performance of the vulnerable other as a sovereign actor endowed with her/his own humanity'. It is through 'theatre' that sufferers' voices can be heard divorced from the subjectivism of pity and irony – that is, arguably freed from Western discourse. How precisely these subalterns are endowed with voice and liberated from Western discourse remains questionable and contestable. The theatrical imagination seems to allow Spivak's subaltern to speak and have a voice. Initially, this is provocative because Spivak's critique of Western, poststructuralist scholars, as discussed at length in chapter 1, is grounded precisely in the charge that they are unable to grasp the importance of difference and how different positions allow some to speak and others to simply repeat. To be sure, Spivak attacks Deleuze and Foucault for rendering invisible their own white, European position and the hegemony it represents. Spivak could arguably level the same critique at Chouliaraki's theatrical imagination.

However, Chouliaraki enlists Michel Foucault's 'Technologies of the Self' (Foucault 1982) to develop the idea of an agonistic space of solidarity or theatrical imagination. In this text, Foucault (224) focusses on the technologies of the self[1] that represent ways of investigating 'truth games' – that is, ways of exploring discourses' public appearances and disappearances in order to understand their functions and meanings as well as their interrelations with contemporary politics and sociality. Technologies of the self are practices or processes of making oneself better. This betterment of the self is not to be construed as a marketisation of the self in which it is the perceived betterment – constructed and controlled by an external public – that is sought. Rather, Foucault's understanding of technologies of the self relies on an understanding of self-improvement that takes its starting point in control over and care for the body and mind. Foucault (234–35) reminds us that the dictum 'know yourself' implies 'care for oneself', and this caring or improvement of oneself is linked to caring for one's political life, indeed to the universal principle of being a better citizen. One technique discussed by Foucault is that of putting oneself in the place of the other, of imagining and thereby training one's mind to cope with suffering. It thus follows that the humanity with which the sufferer is endowed in Chouliaraki's conceptualisation of the theatrical imagination, if further developed with Foucault, becomes a political human – perhaps a citizen. Chouliaraki believes that the practice of theatrical imagination may bring about solidarity and political empathy in an otherwise post-humanitarian world.[2] Chouliaraki's (2013a, 194) position is arguably one of multiple voices from agonistic standpoints: 'Agonism proposes that solidarity is a claim always driven by interests and, consequently, always open to struggle over which of these claims are to be heard and seen, praised or criticized, accepted or rejected'. Taking Spivak's critique into account, it is important to bear in mind whether people taking their positions within the theatrical imagination are aware of and accountable for their respective positions (of power or of resistance). Embodiment and its implications must be continuously invoked in order to create a space of reciprocal respect and to avoid charges of media-centrism. Nevertheless, the theatrical imagination remains for now a political aspiration rather than a reality.

In contrast to the 'participatory culture', the 'DIY citizen' and the 'entertained citizen' of Jenkins, Hartley and van Zoonen, respectively, Chouliaraki emphasises the importance of ethical accountability and investment in mediated citizenship. Whereas the participatory citizen is an intervening citizen, Chouliaraki's theatre approach renders the citizen responsive and responsible. Although her focus is on the specifics of humanitarian communication, her engagement with Foucault may be extended to understand discursive practices of citizenship through media. Taken together, then, the participatory and the performative citizen counterbalance and complement each other's strengths and weaknesses within a common frame of reference that underscores the importance of participation and assumes a citizen aligned with the established deliberative structure of the public. Whereas the performative citizen is responsive and responsible in character, the participatory citizen is intervening and creative. However, rather than engaging with collective solidarity and publics, both approaches relate to the contemporary neo-pragmatic society for which the individual's voice and practice represent the starting point. While theories of media citizenship through participation seem unclear about how to avoid the slippery slope of neo-pragmatist consumerism, Chouliaraki argues that theatrical imagination and empathetic judgement are the answer to the challenges of neo-pragmatism because they allow the individual to imagine the pain of others in a space always open to struggle. Indeed, the very condition of mediated citizenship is arguably that of being able to negotiate fragmented and personalised online politics.

While empathy is undoubtedly vital to political understandings of citizenship and the citizen, I wish to emphasise the necessity of embodying and therefore remembering the political context from which voices emerge and may be heard. Rationally comprehending the other's position and voice is in itself insufficient to break the spell of modernity's categorisations and hierarchies. Embodiment insists on experience and situated memories and thus holds the potential to disrupt and break the frame of the participatory public. In this manner, embodied publics may be constituted outside the participatory framework and truly contribute voice or presence. I return to this argument in the section below: 'The Citizen, the Subject, the Press'.

Virtual Participation

The disembodied notion of political, participatory publics today is emphasised by technology's virtuality. Natalie Fenton (2012) sets forth defining characteristics of the radical publics engaging on the internet. She argues that they are political, highly personalised, populated by the young generations and based on multiplicity and inclusivity. Personalisation and personalised politics and expressions online speak to the idea of the address that generates a public through participation (Warner 2002, Jenkins 2006, Hartley 2012). Rather than an identity-based – often class-based – political struggle, online mediated publics are created through processes of identification and through calls to multiplicity – that is, a large number of known and unknown recipients are called to action or engagement. Online publics of radical politics consist of networked groups with no authoritative figurehead but with a multitude of individuals speaking only for themselves and for a cause that unites them (Fenton 2012). Groups are never homogenous and therefore cannot be led by one person or by the head of an organisation (Isin 2002, Fenton 2012). Whether performative or participatory, this leaves the voice of the individual citizen in a cacophony of causes and multivocality, which the citizen must continuously relate to, amalgamate with or disrupt.

It may be easy to dismiss theories of counterpublics, such as those of Fraser, on account of this new participatory public with all its multitude of voices, particularly following my own approach of mapping the politics of multiple locations. However, I believe it would be a mistake to dismiss Fraser's critique, not only because, without her radical politics in mind, we are left to fend for ourselves with the ultimate neo-pragmatic and ironic (Chouliaraki 2013a) sociality of cyberspace but also because it would – following Spivak's critique – render hegemonic ideologies invisible. I instead wish to insist on the political investment and accountability of the particular positions we inhabit, whether we express these creatively or performatively. Returning to Braidotti's call for deterritorializing identity and politics of location in chapter 1, positions are always situated and embodied, and it is this materialisation of the speech acts, of the performativity, that allows them to be not only empathetic and open but also political and to create a foundation for the 'performer' to become a citizen. It is, then, never enough simply to be exposed to alterity and otherness; situated, political and embodied discourse must continuously circulate, inform and construct the society in which we engage through media (Rothberg 2009, 222). I turn to this argument, which will constitute the basis of my conceptualisation of the citizen in citizen journalism, below.

THE CITIZEN, THE SUBJECT, THE PRESS

For Engin Isin (2002), being political is a relational and affirmative act – that is, a producing act. A citizen acting politically will always act within a given structure relative to or within which she positions herself as opposed or affiliated, while therefore replicating this structure. Affiliating acts within the structure are performative in Judith Butler's (1993) sense of the term – that is, a political practice or policy generating a space or a participatory public. Its reiterative power discursively produces the phenomena that it regulates and constrains. This production is not only discursive but also material. 'To claim that discourse is formative', Butler (10) argues, 'is to claim that there is no pure body which is not at the same time a further formation of that body'. Materialisation is the process through which discourse is stabilised and becomes constitutive of matter over time. The citizen – the material body of the political person – is produced through discursive publics and through the production of a public, but like the performative citizenship theorised by the media theories discussed above, performative citizenship does not produce *acts* of citizenship. Opposing acts – or in Isin's terminology, agon acts – are acts through which the citizen produces 'ruptures from social-historical patterns' (Isin and Nielsen 2008, 11).

> Acts of citizenship are understood as deeds that contain several overlapping and interdependent components. They disrupt habitus, create new possibilities, claim rights and impose obligations in emotionally charged tones; pose their claims in enduring

and creative expressions, and, most of all, are the actual moments that shift established practices, status and order. (10)

While citizenship practices are performative and institutionally accumulated processes (11), acts of citizenship are 'the enactment that transforms a subject into a citizen [and] instantiates a scene in which other subjects are differentiated with the claimant' (18). Acts of citizenship, then, address and call into being a counterpublic while performative citizen practices institutionalise *the* public. It is only in the agonistic space of political acts that the political subject emerges (see also Blaagaard and Roslyng 2016).

Acts of citizenship are acts that are always already embedded in conventions. Performing these conventions without awareness merely reproduces what is already there – that is, what Isin and Nielsen call 'citizenship practices' – while being accountable and responsive through acts brings about citizenship. So, while the citizen comes into being through acts produced within the conventions, it is the intentions and the responsibilities taken in order to produce the act that determine its outcome: success or failure in achieving citizenship (Isin and Ruppert 2015). Following Isin and Ruppert, then, a citizen is a materialised speech act making a rights claim. Isin and Ruppert highlight the importance of awareness and responsibility and thus argue that if we merely repeat speech acts (creative or deliberative) within the already-signified participatory public, we fail in our attempts to become citizens through agency. In order to create a space of agency, we must 'perform our responsibility in re-signifying the conventions by which to act' (60). It is not enough to simply perform: Conventions, habits and modes of expression must be ruptured and given new formats and content. It is, moreover, imperative to consider the territory and the embodiment of the act as well as the intention.

It is worth remarking that all the conceptualisations of citizenship discussed above are achieved – rather than received – citizenship (Dahlgren 2009, 62–63). What Peter Dahlgren calls 'received citizenship' is the legal structure of rights and obligations, whereas 'achieved citizenship' is created through engagements in society. It is the latter that concerns us here, though the two are constantly interrelating: It may be difficult to express and achieve citizenship if one is not entitled to the rights supporting free expression, as Dahlgren (63) argues. In the context of colonies, negotiations of achieved citizenship may lay the foundations for receiving citizenship – or at least Jackson, editor of *The Herald*, seems to have believed the two to be interconnected, as we shall see in chapters 3 and 4.

Historically, received and achieved citizenship can be seen to originate with and be underlined by the transfer of sovereignty from the king to the people, when sovereignty defined by the ruler shifted to popular sovereignty (Balibar 1989, 2004; Dahlgren 2009; Isin 2012). In his influential text from 1989, 'Citizen Subject', Etienne Balibar discusses the question (posed by Jean-Luc Nancy): Who comes after the subject? The subject or *subjectus*, Balibar answers, is the outcome of absolute rule by a sovereign. It is absolutism that brings about the subject, who obeys the ruler. Indeed, Balibar (1989, 40) asserts, obedience is fundamental to the constitution of *subjectus*. An unstable concept, obedience establishes the power asymmetry between the sovereign and the *subjectus*, yet it is the *subjectus* who performs acts of obedience, thereby allowing her to enact power, *subjectum*. Balibar's conception of the subject – *subjectus/subjectum* – can thus be understood in terms of Foucault's technologies of the self, discussed above, as acts of self-improvement, control and obedience. Obedience is not submission but an intentional following of conventions with in-built possibilities of breaking and disrupting these conventions. Isin and Ruppert (2015, 22; emphasis in original, parentheses added) write, 'What distinguishes the citizen from the subject is that the citizen is this composite subject of obedience, submission, and subversion. The birth of the citizen as a *subject of power [subjectum]* does not mean the disappearance of *the subject to power [subjectus]*. The citizen embodies these forms of power'. The citizen follows the subject, writes Balibar (1989, 45, emphasis in original), but the citizen is also 'always a *supposed subject* (legal subject, psychological subject, transcendental subject)'. The citizen subject is then simultaneously the legal, political and cultural citizen enacting, acting and reacting in society. *The Herald*'s concurrent participatory and counterpublic engagements support this nuanced view of the citizen, as will become clear in the following chapters.

The Imagined Community and the Political Citizen

Returning to this chapter's introduction and in light of the colonial settings and possibilities of citizenship as well as the territorial and embodied perspective, the history of the popular sovereignty and the citizen is obviously bound up with the idea of the nation-state. Indeed, Isin (2012) asserts, 'The sovereignty of the people is often expressed only insofar as it claims a state with a territory and it invents nationhood and peoplehood as corresponding entities'. This invention of nationhood, or nation-ness, is the topic of Anderson's *Imagined Communities* (1991). Anderson argues that the nation and its relationships to the idea of the people and race is a historical and discursive construction. It is a construction that supports the idea of the political state by 'always loom[ing] out of an immemorial past . . . and glid[ing] into a limitless future' (Anderson 1991, 11–12). In other words, it is mythological qualities coupled with political force that makes the nation-state so durable and difficult to explain. If we were to follow Gilroy's (2004) suggestion to look at when and where the idea of the nation-state enters into habits and institutions, it is possible to argue that the invention of the nation gives rise to and supports a political force complete with territory, state and a people. That is, the sovereignty of a people and the emergence of the nation-state as territory and peoplehood are interdependent inventions, continuously sustaining each other. However, simply because something is invented or supported by an imaginary does not mean it does not exist, as Isin (2012) astutely puts it. Indeed, '*every social community reproduced by the functioning of institutions is imaginary*' (Balibar 1991, 93, emphasis in original). Isin and Ruppert's (2015) as well as Balibar's arguments above invite us to question the logic of modernity and its understanding of citizenship as inherently connected to identity and community as related to territory. They also make clear that media theories of participatory and performative publics and citizens are inherent to citizenship formations but are ultimately inadequate to understanding the embodied nature of political citizenship. The theories reiterated above identify the discursive imagined structures of citizenship and community. Nevertheless, the one aspect of the imagined national community that makes it nearly impenetrable remains the role of the press (Anderson 1991, 61).

The continuous reproduction of the imagined community is not static. For instance, Isin (2012) reads Foucault to gain an understanding of how and when the bourgeoisie went from enacting their position as *a* nation among other class-related nations to becoming *the* nation and in this manner produced the foundations of the nationally bound nation-state, supported by print capitalism. However, through the provinciality and plurality of local, colonial newspapers, print capitalism may be said to have provided a counterbalance in Spanish-speaking America, where the unification of territory did not occur through common language. Reading Anderson's theory of print capitalism alongside Foucault's and Balibar's citizen subject, although print capitalism arguably provided new fixity to the language through which an asymmetrical relationship was performed, print capitalism also created a possibility for disruption of these soon-to-be powerful conglomerates of news production and distribution. Indeed, Jackson's *The Herald* may be presented as an example of how print capitalism gave rise both to political acts of citizenship and to cosmopolitan connections between people who were citizens of no nation-state, between fragmented and dispersed entities of commonality.

What is at stake is the idea of 'the people' – because it is the people who continually (re)construct the imagined community of the nation-state (Balibar 1991, 93). The people is not a static category either but is a constant and continuing production. Indeed, if Anderson sees nationalism in an anthropological light and as a cultural imaginary akin to religious movements, Balibar (96) argues further that it is through fictive or fabricated ethnicity that national ideology may interpellate individuals into an imagined community of belonging. Fictive ethnicities are constructed through language and race. The idea of a national common language is, like nationalism, produced through tales of the national language as ancient and natural; however, as in the case of nations, national languages are a recent invention. Translators of the modern world are journalists, politicians and social actors, who produce the language of the people, as discussed above (Anderson 1991, Balibar 1991). But the language community is insufficient to support the fictive notion of ethnicity. In contrast to communication and language, race is based on the idea of generations carrying inherited communities within, which is why the naturalisation of the nation through myths of common ancestry and extended kinship always already brings us in the presence of the category of race (Balibar 1991, 100). It is, then, the case that 'the people', the body of citizen subjects, are held together and continuously produce the imaginary nation-state through discourses of journalistic and social translation as well as structures of population politics, such as genealogies and extended kin. The implications of this are mirrored in the colonial history itself and make it possible for states to emphasise the coherency of the nation-state's identity even when its borders are extended to encompass colonised territory, thereby driving racist historicism and naturalisations. Citizens and subjects may be able to participate in this construction through journalism in the participatory public, but as I have argued with the help of Fraser, if the public is continuously theorised as an egalitarian space in which debates concerning 'common good' take place between similar identities and positions, participation merely reproduces the predetermined national interests and, therefore historically, the interests of the white bourgeoisie.

Objectivity and Digital Media

The theories that I have rehearsed above all to varying degrees presuppose a common space in which all – bourgeoisie and subaltern alike – may be heard and listened to. Indeed, such a space would ultimately be capable of challenging the status quo of postcolonial power relations. What is needed, these theories argue, are political strategies for learning to listen. What is truly needed, however, is not just a strategy for learning to listen[3] but also a challenge to the very assumption of the public sphere; the participatory public; and the role of journalism, language and race in the construction of the nation-state and national identity. I seek to transcend the arguably privileged position of being able to decide to listen, and I instead argue for a rethinking of public space and citizen agency by taking a different perspective, one that does not favour already established ideas of national coherency and journalism. Understanding citizen journalism through readings of the postcolonial case of *The Herald* forces us to think public space and citizenship anew by challenging the idea of the common good and the boundaries of the nation-state. We need to bring the concept of cosmopolitanism into the discussion.

Ideas regarding journalism's cosmopolitan values are being reinvigorated by acknowledgement of the world's increasing interdependence, globalisation and a concomitantly produced range of normative guidelines as to how social policy and intervention may help achieve a more just world (Fine 2007, Held 2004). As mentioned in chapter 1, technology was historically seen as supporting objectivity because it helped regulate linguistically expressed human biases. Journalism is favoured as a marker of free democratic publics, while technology connects people's minds and ideas and promotes equality due to its inherent neutrality: Technology and journalism combined may aid in the global spread of the modern idea of the public sphere and its deliberative model when understood as a political – but technologically virtual – space in which we all interact on equal terms. In this way, the public sphere expands into a globally spanning realm of citizenship, as a mode of political cosmopolitanism supported by the practice of journalism, while glossing over inherent inequalities and differences.

Following this idea of objectivity-*cum*-cosmopolitanism, a persistent argument in both journalism scholarship and journalistic practice holds that a free press is pivotal to achieving justice and equality on a global scale through objectivity, truth seeking and impartiality (Beckett 2008, 8). Although no doubt an alluring argument, political positioning remains key, as in the case of the participatory public and the theatrical imagination. The argument flies in the face of Fraser's, Warner's and Isin's conceptualisations of publics and citizenship, discussed above. Moreover, cosmopolitanism has been discussed in critical terms. In particular, its propensity for universalism and rationalism has been challenged by postcolonial theories, continental philosophies and radical politics of difference (Braidotti, Hanafin and Blaagaard 2013). Objectivity, moreover, remains a contested journalistic principle (Blaagaard 2013, Boudana 2011, Hampton 2008, Tuchman 1972, Wahl-Jørgensen 2012, Ward 2008). Nevertheless, the connection between technology, objectivity and cosmopolitan sensibilities is a recurrent theme in communication and journalism studies, especially when new technologies emerge and make new claims of connectivity and social relations between global spaces, such as in the case of digital and social media and citizen journalism. Media analysts and theorists such as Jay Rosen (2008) and Dan Gillmor (2004) attest to this view. For instance, Rosen's definition of citizen journalism is 'when citizens exchange information via digital media, whereas civic journalism depends on professional journalists to create and frame the exchange'. My argument here is that citizen journalism is not just a matter of information exchange among citizens; the information and the exchange need to have a political grounding. The citizen of citizen journalism needs to enact her citizenship, so to speak, so that citizenship is achieved rather than received. This definition in turn calls for a different conceptualisation of cosmopolitanism, because grounding in a particular culture or place may prove challenging for a citizen of the world.

In the remainder of this chapter, I develop a way of thinking about citizen journalism outside national identity and borders.

COLONIALISM, COSMOPOLITANISM AND DETERRITORIALIZATIONS

In chapters 3 and 4, I produce close readings of *The Herald*, particularly Jackson's editorial and journalistic work as well as his activist work in constructing a labour union. These readings politically situate Jackson in an assemblage of diverse and multidirectional strategies and imaginaries. In the context of this chapter, it is worthwhile repeating that while there is no doubt that Jackson addressed a particular public and had ambitions on its behalf, through its ten years of publication, *The Herald* alternated between, on the one hand, being a political act of citizenship that countered the Danish mainstream public and, on the other hand, being a publication that aspired to entering *the* public sphere, trying to perform a role of the educational and informational press. *The Herald* defies several histories of journalism and of citizenship, and through this resistance to identification and fixity, concepts of citizen journalism emerge.

As described in the introduction to this chapter, despite being published in a Danish colony, *The Herald* was written in English. But language itself may determine cultural connections that stretched far beyond the colonial region. While shared language underscores the national 'we', discontinuities of language (Hannerz 1996, 21) – that is, the fact that *The Herald* and the press in general on the islands were printed in English rather than Danish – potentially produced local difference and simultaneously connection to elsewhere, rather than to the colonial power and culture of Denmark. In this manner, *The Herald* highlights the shifting, contracting and expanding boundaries of culture. In a term coined by anthropologist Ulf Hannerz (1996, 22), *The Herald* may be seen as producing a 'habitat of meaning'. Habitats of meaning are the continuously changing sum of (global and local) connections and knowledges of an individual or collective. 'Our habitats of meaning will of course depend not only on what in some physical sense we are exposed to, but also on the capabilities we have built up for coping with it knowledgeably: the languages we understand, write, or speak, our levels of literacy with respect to symbolic forms, and so on' (23). Habitats of meaning thus moreover require education and information flow and may through this span the 'global ecumene', which is Hannerz's (23) preferred term for what others might term another cosmopolitan space (Benhabib 2006).

The global, Hannerz argues, is the marker of change, and the local is connected to continuity and familiarity. Hannerz explains how the local is characterised by face-to-face interactions, early formative experiences and sensorial and bodily experiences. The local is where our experiences are contextualised and make sense to us. This is what I in chapter 1 called 'situatedness' and which I connected to how citizen journalism draws upon affective and bodily connections as well as political implications (see also Blaagaard 2013a). However, Hannerz also argues that media may help generate similar experiences and contexts in non-shared physical spaces. Again, we may question the assumptions of the local as opposed to the global by looking at *The Herald* and the habitat of meaning it produced, connecting to African American political activists as well as to Danish progressives. In the following two chapters, I will argue that this is precisely what *The Herald* achieved: expanding the habitat of meaning of the African Caribbean people of St. Croix to recognise their familiarity and common culture with both the socialist progressive movement in Denmark and the burgeoning civil rights movement in the United States. *The Herald* may thus be seen as producing a cosmopolitan space and practice. 'In identifying the typical components of localness, we may also come to realize more clearly that they are not intrinsically local, linked to territoriality in general or only some one place in particular. That connection is really made rather by recurrent practicalities of life, and by habits of thought' (Hannerz 1996, 27). Ideologies or cultural connections may then act as local experiences while transcending territory and historical time. Socialism and feminism as movements, for example, are known to have no commitment to any one country.[4] Similarly, the African American communities in New York provided Jackson with a shared experience of diaspora beyond national boundaries.

To my mind, the difference between Hannerz's global ecumene, which marks the horizon of habitats of meaning, and legal-political cosmopolitan space, as theorised by authors such as Benhabib, lies not only in their disciplinary traditions and terminology but also in their actual political implications. While Benhabib necessarily takes a starting point within the borders of nation-states and the politico-legal status of citizenship, Hannerz's anthropological and social science explorations do not necessitate such limitations. Pitching cosmopolitanism as a political player in global market structures, Benhabib (2007, 22) sees cosmopolitanism as a potential critique of capitalist self-interest, while Hannerz's strength lies in his focus on cultural practices and social meaning-making, which circumscribe structural politics. But it is exactly Benhabib's connection to concepts of state and popular sovereignty that allows her to see the legal and political struggles of peoples and of habitats of meaning. As with Gilroy, it is through popular sovereignty that struggles of representation and rights are built and fought, Benhabib (23) argues. People may engage in 'complex processes of public argument, deliberation, and exchange through which universalist rights claims and principles are contested and contextualized' (31). These are what Benhabib (31) calls 'democratic iterations', in which every repetition is a variation. The iterative acts allow people to re-signify and attach new meaning to norms and regulations through participation. As an example, Benhabib (2006) discusses the French public debates concerning the Muslim headscarf that swept through the nation of France in the 1990s. The debates began with three Muslim girls being sent home from school because they had covered their hair, and the developing discussions ended up challenging French rights and freedom of religion. The schoolgirls re-signified what it meant to wear the headscarf, argues Benhabib (56), and placed the French state in the paradoxical position of *dictating* more autonomy. Thus, '[d]emocratic iterations can lead to processes of public self-reflection as well as generating public defensiveness' (61). Gilroy finds the solution to sustaining embodied participation and intervention in cosmopolitan politics by revisiting the issue of race. Without acknowledging modernity's racial structures and their implications, we will continue to resort to 'a Manichaean fantasy in which bodies are only ordered and predictable units' (Gilroy 2004, 6). That is, a rupture of memory is necessary for accomplishing cosmopolitan conviviality. The two scholars' positions mirror the two possibilities of political subjectivity advanced in this chapter: participatory and performative versus political, though on the level of the global cosmopolitan.

While Benhabib does not distinguish between re-significations that rupture norms and regulations – such as in the case of the French debates – and those that simply sustain the already-defined common good, I believe that the concept of 'acts of citizenship' (Isin and Nielsen 2008) is helpful here. Democratic iterations refer to universal rights and norms, while acts of citizenship not only promise change but also rely upon a far more grounded conceptualisation of rights. That is, Isin and Nielsen maintain the dual movement of governmentality and technology through which citizens operate in national as well as cosmopolitan contexts. For Isin and Nielsen, rights claims grow out from cultural signification based on habitats of meaning that may span several continents and national jurisdictions but are significant to a particular setting and experience. That means that the concept of cosmopolitan relations, following Hannerz as well as Isin and Nielsen, is based on collective or communal engagements rather than individual iterations. Another glance at the concept of deterritorialization may likewise prove useful here. In the previous chapter, supported by Deleuze and Guattari (1994), I discussed how deterritorialization is part of political movements signifying relational politics of location. Benhabib (2007, 25–26) uses the term to argue that territory and legal regulations are decoupled, underscoring multinational, capitalist ventures and leaving citizens at a legal loss. For Deleuze and Guattari, however, deterritorialization is part of an affirmative process of re-signification and uprooting, simultaneously resembling Benhabib's democratic iterations and Isin and Nielsen's acts of citizenship. That is, the concept is accompanied by political rupture and change. In this manner, it is helpful to delink the analysis from notions of states and institutions while retaining the significance of geography and the political.

Cosmopolitanism and City Journalism

Bringing these definitions back to the practice of journalism or citizen journalism, Benhabib neglects to mention the role of the press when focussing on the French headscarf affair. As a practice that in itself may be understood as a democratic iteration of the right to a free press and free speech, the role of journalism seems awkwardly absent from her analysis. How may we think of journalistic practice as well as the significance of space and time yet do so outside the realm of the nation-state and its institutions?

Terhi Rantanen's (2007) answer is that it is a mistake to begin explorations of journalistic practice by drawing upon its relationship to the nation-state. Rantanen instead diverges from the prevalent idea of the nation-state as a starting point for journalistic news and argues that the mistake originates in the emergence of modern journalism, which coincided with an emphasis on the modern nation-state. Rejecting the established theories of the press's role in creating and sustaining the imagined national community (Anderson 1991), Rantanen believes that journalism was a product embedded in cities and, moreover, in cities that were connected through the technology of the printing press. Rantanen (2007, 843–45) therefore seeks to understand journalistic news as rooted in cosmopolitan cities. Rantanen's concept of cosmopolitanization of news builds upon Hannerz's habitats of meaning and global ecumene, discussed above. She furthermore recognises the political role of journalism and thereby imbues Hannerz's cultural connections with political potential. Whereas cosmopolitans are often – even by Hannerz – understood as belonging to a certain socioeconomic class, holding privileges of knowledge and ability, 'the same abilities can be found in individuals who resist the existing world order and are critical of it. They are not necessarily members of the dominant elite, but often excluded from it because of their race, ideology or religion' (847). Following these theorists' thinking, it is through the very practice of journalism – albeit in counter-narrative and disruptive form – that citizens occupying certain habitats of meaning within the global ecumene may act politically. Indeed, we may perhaps speak of a deterritorialization of news and journalism. Rantanen's shift in journalistic-historical focus from the nation to the city opens up our thinking to the possibility of looking beyond reiterative and performative acts. Looking beyond established knowledge of the performative power of journalism, moreover, creates cracks through which another narrative, told by other citizens, may become available. This perspective invites citizens' political acts because it lays the groundwork for other assertions, expressions and claims, made using other formats and voices.

CITIZEN JOURNALISM DECONSTRUCTED

Beginning from *The Herald*'s three challenges of language, race and territory and moving to journalism's role within the construction of the nation-state, I have argued in this chapter that the citizen of citizen journalism is produced through an act of citizenship that disrupts the performed practices of citizenship associated with received citizenship and deliberations within the national public sphere. The citizen is becoming-citizen, meaning that it is a continuous and creative process driven by political agency. Delinked from a definition determined by professional journalism, the citizen of citizen journalism generates another kind of public, one based on political and cultural habitats of meaning and therefore embodied and situated. This kind of definition of the citizen of citizen journalism departs from theorisations that take their starting point in participation and Habermas's public sphere. Moreover, I have argued that journalism offers a potential for not only producing acts of citizenship but also for connecting habitats of meaning that are based in global cities or regions, within the global ecumene. Citizenship is thus now an act, and journalism is a political practice linking habitats of meaning. Decoupling journalism from the nation-state and the public sphere offers it far greater potential, so journalism can be understood in terms of affirmative production of publics and subjectivity formation. Delinked from the modern conceptualisation, room for diversity emerges as a movement of deterritorialization: Citizen journalism may be produced by citizens overlooked and disregarded within the modern nation-state context of the history of journalism and citizenship. It is not just a question of listening but also of tuning in to a different beat. This does not necessarily mean that practices of participation through creative coproduction or DIY projects are obsolete or non-political. To the contrary, creative processes of breaking the moulds of mainstream media may be part of political acts and may under certain circumstances be understood as citizen journalism. Chouliaraki's performative and aesthetic publicness, with its focus on affectivity and playfulness, may be the basis on which political acts are generated. Chapter 5 will look at the role of the visual and aesthetics more closely. What is important to the concept of the citizen in citizen journalism as defined here is the political engagement and struggle for social change as well as the embodied experience of a counter-position.

Chapter 3 applies this conceptualisation of the citizen to the first of two close readings of *The Herald*.

NOTES

1. The four kinds of technology identified by Foucault are: (1) technologies of production, (2) technologies of signs, (3) technologies of power and (4) technologies of the self. Whereas the first two kinds of technology relate to his work on the sciences and linguistics, the last two relate to the subject and subjectivities. It is the last two technologies that are of interest here. In particular, technologies of the self are drawn upon by much work on media, journalism and citizenship.

2. Chouliaraki's (2013a) theory of post-humanitarianism is laid out in her book *The Ironic Spectator*.

3. I am, moreover, not entirely convinced that it is possible to bring about such a strategy beyond persistent power relations and historical suppression.

4. However, Gilroy argues (2004, 5) that rather than extending commitments beyond borders, in the process of breaking down the national boundaries of political culture, socialism fostered a disaffection from those who were close by.

3

Political Citizen Journalism

Cosmopolitanism and Citizenship in Colonies

In 1915, political agitator, schoolteacher and lawyer, David Hamilton Jackson, travelled from St. Croix to Denmark, the then-colonial power of the Caribbean islands currently known as the United States Virgin Islands. Jackson did so to argue for his right to free speech and print, to argue for his right to publish *The Herald*. Over the ten years that followed, Jackson's work as *The Herald*'s editor, publisher and reporter engaged with the islands' African-Caribbean people as citizens. Although arguably colonial subjects who lacked rights and benefits afforded to legal citizens, the practices of Jackson's journalism, particularly the practice of selecting and bringing together journalistic products from New York and Copenhagen news, nevertheless constituted a way of addressing a public, whereby its readers were called upon to act as political citizens. Focusing on these citizen-making practices of journalism as foundational to the concept of citizen journalism, this chapter theoretically draws upon and advances the previous chapter, which elaborated upon acts of citizenship (cf. Isin 2002, Isin and Nielsen 2008, Isin and Ruppert 2015) as constitutional to publics and counterpublics (Fraser 1990). Isin (2002, 32) argues that publics are relational, and he defines 'being political' as a relationship that can be either one of affiliation (i.e., sameness and recognition) or one of agon and estrangement. Using empirical examples from *The Herald*, I argue that these kinds of political acts and creations of counterpublics are indicative of (post)colonial struggles for citizenship and subjectivity, such as those of Jackson and his peers.

This chapter tells the story in the words of David Hamilton Jackson of *The Herald*'s positioning in the colonial society of St. Croix, St. Thomas and St. John. The intricate links between political movements and citizens' rights claims within and beyond the paper are meticulously reported by Jackson and his peers in *The Herald*. The ten years of publication present movements of de- and reterritorialization, which will be further discussed in the chapters to come. The present chapter, moreover, discusses how practices of citizenship and addressing a public operate across borders and cultural boundaries, linking citizens to one another in a cultural cosmopolitanism. This chapter's cartographic analysis draws extensively upon the theories discussed in chapters 1 and 2, in which connectivity is divorced from technology, and the argument of technology's neutrality and journalistic objectivity's global scope are refuted. In the present chapter, I show how Jackson often brings together writings by New York–based political activists and writers of the early civil rights movement and the African American minority press as well as translated opinion pieces and political debates from Danish newspapers. In this way, *The Herald* functions as a place of connectivity or cosmopolitanism, understood in terms of connecting distant corners of the world without the use of physical transport or technological transmission but by building a cultural and political 'bridge' between a distinct 'here' and a distinct 'there' (Rantanen 2003, 436) – that is, between Copenhagen, New York and the Virgin Islands. This kind of cosmopolitan practice relies on the idea of phenomenological geography, which concerns 'people's own experience, how they feel about places' (437). By sharing and creating experiences through translations and reprints, the pages of *The Herald* constitute a phenomenological space in which a cosmopolitan public is addressed and produced, rendering the newspaper an example of citizen journalism. This is, in other words, the recirculation of discourse that allows a counterpublic to emerge. Next, the cultural practice of 'poaching' (Jenkins 1992) is explored and suggested as a term for the particular journalistic cultural and cosmopolitan practice that supported Jackson's political act of addressing a cosmopolitan public. Finally, the chapter shows how the terms on which *The Herald* based its political practice related to and brought about shifting territorializations over the course of its ten years of print. The chapter tells the story of a counterpublic in the making, of the twists and turns it produced.

Methodologically, the chapter relies upon a critical, discursive reading introduced as the book's framework in chapter 1. The reading focusses on *The Herald*, 1915–1925, as well as the historical context in which the paper was produced and published. In this manner, the chapter seeks to mirror and elaborate upon chapter 2 by developing the argument empirically. First, I focus on the editions of *The Herald* published before the Virgin Islands were sold to the United States, that is, 1915–1916. As the islands were transferred to US jurisdiction, new battles for citizenship and belonging emerged in the paper, and the ecology of the public shifted. The cartographic analysis of *The Herald* proceeds as a mapping out of (post)colonial interconnections between geographical spaces, political ideas and embodied experiences, bringing about a reading against the grain (Braidotti 2011). I advance the critical argument presented in chapter 1 against the oft-cited idea of contemporary citizen journalism as determined by its relationship to professional journalistic practice and technological developments. Considering the political agency of citizen journalism from a cultural-historical perspective, rather than in light of today's fascination with the digital, enables me to see how communication technology and publication practices have worked on levels of engagements to strengthen citizens' voices and commitments in counterpublic and border-crossing communities in a historical context. This redefinition of citizen journalism outside the institutional press is supported in this case because *The Herald* was published when the institutionalisation of journalism was still in its infancy and in a colony – that is, a region that questions the boundaries of the nation-state. Whereas theories of mediatisation argue for the importance of technological developments to social relations, and journalism studies tends to focus on the technological possibilities of dissemination and amplification underlying practices of citizen journalism (see Allan 2013, Allan and Thorsen 2009), this chapter shows how a redefinition of citizen journalism might look in terms of citizens' engagements with publics via publication strategies and of lived experiences and political practices. These practices may be widely disseminated due to technology, but it is the sense of experiencing proximity and shared space and belonging that holds the potential for cosmopolitan journalism. I now continue my questioning of the concept of the citizen, which I began in chapter 2, followed by a repositioning in relation to the idea of journalism, and I end by arguing for an embodied, political practice.

JACKSON'S POLITICAL ACT

In order to contextualise *The Herald* as an example of citizen-making practice and thereby redefine citizen journalism by shifting perspectives, I start by presenting part of Danish colonial history, with continual reference to the empirical reading as I draw upon theoretical accounts. As mentioned in previous chapters, *The Herald* was the initiative of Jackson, a political agitator, socialist and descendant of enslaved workers. Jackson argued that the Danish colonial administration enact social reforms and grant him the right to publish *The Herald*. His requests for reforms – including workers' rights to own land, inclusion of black gendarmes in the gendarmerie and the dismissal of the governor – were denied, but the law demanding royal permission to publish was subsequently withdrawn, and Jackson was allowed to print the first independent newspaper in the Caribbean colony (Hoxcer Jensen 1981).

Over the course of approximately two hundred fifty years of Danish colonial history,[1] more than one hundred ten thousand African enslaved people were forced to relocate to the Caribbean islands. Continuously, they rebelled and fought back through revolts and the so-called fireburns.[2] Ultimately, and during another large-scale revolt, the Danish governor, Peter von Scholten, saw no way out but to proclaim on 3 July 1848 the emancipation of the enslaved people. Even after the abolition of slavery, working conditions for the islands' labourers were extremely hard. As in many colonial societies, unequal power structures remained after slavery was abolished. Generations later, Jackson, who was the son of a schoolteacher and who himself taught local schoolchildren and later pursued a career as a lawyer, became editor and writer of *The Herald*. Jackson was known locally as a political agitator, who criticised inequalities in education, the failings of the healthcare provision and hospitals, and the inadequate exchange of information between landowners and labourers. To this day, he is remembered and celebrated on St. Croix, particularly on Liberty Day, 1 November, and prominent statues represent him in town squares in Christiansted, St. Croix. Jackson visited Denmark several times and gave public talks there. His visits were publicised and featured in Danish newspapers as well as in *The Herald*.

The Herald was part of a process of political engagement aimed at improving working conditions on the islands through education, information and deliberation. The first issue of *The Herald* was published and distributed on 29 October 1915, having been produced by the United Danish West Indian Printing Plant Corporation, which was funded by social democratic parties in Denmark and floating bonds in New York. In the very first edition of *The Herald*, Jackson stated:

> With many apologies we today send forth our first little printed sheet, with the hope that its readers will find in it what was long wanted – a paper for the people. . . . A certain great writer once said 'Give to the people what they want and there shall be no discontent'. –We want our people to have all they are entitled to as citizens. (31.10.15)

The Herald was not just a newspaper. From the very first issue, focus was placed on acquiring civic and labour rights for the islands' labourers. These labourers were predominantly African Caribbean people directly descended from the enslaved workers who had gained their freedom only a few generations prior to the publication of *The Herald*. The role of the press was pivotal to achieving workers' rights, and Jackson was explicit about this in his endeavour to speak up for the labourers.

Up until 1915, the only papers published in the three Danish Caribbean colonies had been produced by the Danish administration. The only other two newspapers being published at the time were *The St. Croix Avis* (the official government paper, which had been published under various names since 1770 and which still exists today as an independent paper) and *The West End News* (which had existed on the island since 1912 and within which Jackson himself had previously agitated extensively). Ideologically, *The Herald* was linked to the social democratic labour movement and displayed in its heading the slogan 'liberty–equality–fraternity'. This obvious reference to a major citizens' uprising and to a democratic agenda highlights Jackson's call for citizen participation in social and political change and his emphasis on personal (educational) change. Moreover, social democratic Danish papers, such as *Socialdemokraten* and *Politiken*, were mentioned in the first edition of *The Herald* as supporters of the political and journalistic cause. Clearly, for Jackson, *The Herald* was a participatory means to a political end, as his first editorial address places responsibility for the island's future in the hands and pages of *The Herald*.

However, *The Herald* was not met with delight on all sides. Despite having gained the right to print his paper, Jackson encountered hostility back on the island as rumours spread among plantation owners that he was returning with plans for political revolt. Word was sent to Denmark to send the military vessel *Valkyrien* as soon as possible in order 'to quell imaginary disturbance' (30.11.15). In a piece translated from Danish and previously published in the Danish newspaper *Politiken*, it was reported that a telegram from the La Grange plantation had urged the Danish government to send a warship and two hundred men because uprising was imminent (29.11.15). Jackson also sent a telegram of his own to his friend and member of Danish parliament (the Folketinget), Hans Nielsen, recounting the mistreatment of the labourers and threats to close down his newspaper by white administrators and landowners on the island. The tensions and disputes were reported as far away as in the *New York Evening Journal* (2.12.15). It is, therefore, possible to assume that as tensions on the islands escalated, Jackson's reporting of the situation was aimed at a public that was wider and more diverse than that of St. Croix itself. He placed the local situation in a wider political context. Jackson wrote:

> Since our return [from Denmark] we have been holding mass meetings all over the island and in St. Thomas for the purpose of giving an understanding of our work among the blacks in these waters. In all these movements we have had and are still having a pack of dogs at our heels barking incessantly, and others were venturing to cry out 'Stop him! Stop him! Won't somebody stop him? Something must be done to stop him!' (2.12.15)

The public Jackson addressed when recounting the pressure and threats he must endure to publish the newspaper consisted of not only the local population but also New Yorkers and Danes in Copenhagen. Jackson was documenting his and the people's story and stance for the Danish administration and political peers as well as for potential political allies in New York and Denmark. The public *per* Warner is self-organising and must thus address peers and strangers alike. The pressure did not let up: Officials and administrative staff soon began bringing lawsuits against the paper and against Jackson. *The Herald* reported that the *Valkyrien* arrived in St. Croix on 9 December 1915, noting satirically, however, that, despite the rumoured revolt, the governor was not on the island at the time. Regardless of all the threats, no violence was ever reported.

The Herald was not born into an easy or welcoming environment. Indeed, *The Herald* may be regarded as a form of resistance within a community dominated by white plantation owners, who responded to this resistance by issuing warnings of revolt and calling on reinforcements from Denmark. Furthermore, the environment was not merely local but also connected to New York and Copenhagen as well as to international streams of political ideology. Jackson's political and journalistic work in *The Herald* may be characterised as 'ruptures from social-historical patterns' (Isin and Nielsen 2008, 11) because of its social and political display of community building by addressing the African Caribbean people in colonies as political subjects and a public. The concept of 'a public' is here taken from Michael Warner's (2002) discussion of 'publics' and 'counterpublics', discussed in chapter 1. Warner builds upon the work of Nancy Fraser (1990) and emphasises the deconstructive mode of counter-political social movements such as feminist, LGBTQI (lesbian, gay, bisexual, transgender, queer or questioning and intersex), and antiracist movements. The basis of these counterpublics is the availability of recirculated discourses of shared convictions, which in turn clash with *the* public. Indeed, Fraser's (61) lucid take on the concept of the public defines a counterpublic as in conflict with the public.

Fraser (67) describes 'subaltern counterpublics' as '[p]arallel discursive arenas where members of subordinated social groups invent and circulate counter-discourses, which in turn permits them to formulate oppositional interpretations of their identities, interests, and needs.' Thus, *The Herald*'s publication – in which Jackson addressed the specific social, political and educational needs of the African Caribbean population through articles on healthcare, child minding and daily vocabulary and reading lists for the education of the people – may be seen as a discursive counterpublic. Furthermore, Engin Isin (2002) conceptualises social groups in terms of address and the concomitant recognition of that address (Warner 2002), which in turn generates the group or public.

Isin, moreover, identifies not just the individual actor or agent addressing and calling into being a public but also the singular political act as a point of analytical as well as political interest. Through his political and educational writings in *The Herald*, Jackson addressed the African Caribbean people as a particular community, not as opposed to but in agonistic relation to the colonial power. That is, although Jackson had legally obtained the right to publish his newspaper from the Danish government, and although he often wrote admiringly of Danish freedoms and press, he also quite clearly addressed the racial and social problems of colonial society: It is these addresses that I argue are citizen journalistic. For example, on 1 November 1915, in the second published issue of *The Herald*, the paper warned that 'THE CIRCULAR sent out by the AGRICULTURAL EXPERIMENT STATION, should not be taken as applying to the SMALL SQUATTER.' Squatters, who were comprised of the African Caribbean population, should not sign anything that they did not understand, the warning continued. The circular was meant for the planters – that is, the predominantly white plantation owners on the islands. This dispute escalated into a full-blown strike by February the following year.[3] Similarly, a case of possible wrongful confiscation of a man's firearm by the gendarmerie in mid-November 1915 led Jackson to question the lawfulness of the gendarmerie altogether: 'In fact the people ought to know something about these gendarmes and their connections with the civil authorities' (11.1.15), he wrote, hinting that the gendarmerie's legal functions on the island were at best ambiguous to the paper and the people. These were all long-held political projects of Jackson's. Jackson placed himself within the category of 'the people', and this affiliation is at times stronger and more racially explicit: 'The people' are the black labourers, descendants of enslaved workers, at least during the early years of publication and before the islands were transferred to US jurisdiction. The inner legal and political workings of labourers' daily lives and their relationships with the colonisers on the colonial islands were contested but not denied.

Here, again, Isin is helpful: Isin (2002, 30) finds it important to distinguish between what he calls 'logics of alterity', which constitute immanent strangers and aliens, from 'the logic of exclusion', which creates 'barbarians' as exterior entities (30). In *The Herald*, the Danish colonizers were not portrayed as outsiders to the African Caribbean 'squatters' or counterpublic, which the paper addressed, as the above examples testify. Instead, *The Herald* took a 'relational approach' (29–30) in addressing the colonizers and the public. This approach involved more than just a shift from an understanding of the colonial public as unitary and unified to an understanding based on an underdog position on the part of *The Herald* and Jackson. The two understandings may no longer be meaningfully separated but ultimately interact and interchange in everyday life. By conceptualising the political act through which a public emerges, Jackson's desire and eventual ability to produce *The Herald* as well as *The Herald*'s content may be construed as a political act calling upon an African Caribbean public of political subjects, if not legal citizens, in the colonies. This public includes Jackson himself. Let us unpack this claim.

The Herald emerged within an international multiplicity of publications, counterpublics, politics and social progressiveness, including a wide range of journals and papers addressing African American and general female publics. These were a result of cheaper production costs on paper, changes in postal taxes, the telegraph and widespread literacy. As described in the previous chapter, in the United States, journalism was only just beginning to undergo a professionalisation in terms of organisation, training and ideology: The institutionalisation of the press was not yet clear-cut. In Denmark, the four major newspapers carried essays as well as lyrical reports and short news, but the practice of interviews and objectivity had not been fully implemented (cf. Jensen 1997). As a publication separate from the local, colonial politics of the time, *The Herald* took its place among many other politically charged publications (that were distinct from the mainstream and professional publications) in both Copenhagen and New York. They were journals and papers that opined on women's rights, common people's right to education and sexual liberty, the civil rights of African Americans, and arts and education. Such publications included titles such as *Korsaren* and *Klingen* in Denmark and titles such as *The Truthseeker*, *The Path Finder*, and *The Crisis* in the United States. Jackson engaged with these diverse publications and cosmopolitan people and places in different modalities: First, much as digital communication online is claimed to spark revolutions in the Middle East, *The Herald* amplifies Jackson's socialist politics and union work and helps make visible the networks and causes for which he worked. This was achieved simply by addressing a part of the population that had not previously been addressed through the papers published by the colonial administration on the island. By agitating, educating and informing his readers about the specific issues of their livelihoods and working conditions as well as announcing when and where he would speak live in public, where people could congregate, Jackson addressed his peers and readers as a public. By reading *The Herald* and meeting physically, readers responded to the address. Second, the networking quality of *The Herald* incorporated and recirculated writings both by people engaged in New York's burgeoning Harlem Renaissance and early civil rights politics as well as by political progressives in both Denmark and New York. In the United States, these were not white progressives, who, as shall be argued below, despite their social awareness were subject to the telegraph's commercialisation and the consequent invisibility of cultural and racial minorities in the United States (Gonzáles and Torres 2011). This was instead the work of people such as Ida B. Wells, who wrote searing commentaries and reports on the racial inequality of US segregation policies. In Denmark, progressives argued for social change and sexual liberties through widespread education. These Danish progressives also supported Jackson and his newspaper, though decolonisation was discussed only sporadically in the Danish public sphere. *The Herald*, then, contained and related to pieces and politics on everyday practices, such as school, chores, education, child rearing and vocabulary training as well as news about local and colonial politics, the gendarmerie and rum shops. These practices were moreover acts of political substance inasmuch as they called self-organized publics into existence. Although it had a socialist leaning, the paper was not an anti-colonial or antagonistic paper but represented a continuous politically agonistic act that related to the (colonial) political everyday workings of the islands at the time as well as to the experiences and politics of similar publics in Copenhagen and New York.

As described above, in Isin's terminology, agon acts are acts through which the citizen produces breaks from mainstream and historically contingent patterns (Isin and Nielsen 2008, 10–11): Acts of citizenship are 'deeds' of 'several overlapping and interdependent components', which disrupt, create, and claim rights as well as impose obligations through their shifts away from established practices and toward new creative and disruptive possibilities.

While citizenship practices are performative and institutionally accumulated processes (Isin and Nielsen 2008, 11), acts of citizenship are 'the enactment that transforms a subject into a citizen [and] instantiates a scene in which other subjects are differentiated with the claimant' (Isin and Nielsen 2008, 18). Acts of citizenship, then, address and call into being a public, or a counterpublic, while performative citizen practices institutionalise the public, as discussed in chapter 2. It is only in the agonistic space of political acts that the political subject emerges. Jackson produced an act of citizenship when he addressed and called into being an African Caribbean public in St. Croix, yet *The Herald* was also a performative practice of citizenship, granting the islands' African Caribbean majority a common space of deliberation. Here is Jackson at length in his opening editorial (31.10.15):

> It is not our intention to antagonize any existing paper or journal, but we certainly are in the field to defend the darker race from attacks by the papers, journals or journalists opposed to their progress – the march toward their heritage.
> If we were to tell the truth in its fullness about the present condition of the island then we should unhesitatingly lay the blame to the inactivity of the Press. Let us go back to the time when the common people in Denmark had no paper or organ of their own and what do we find there? oppression and semi-slavery. [. . .] It is through the spread of newspaper literature that Denmark has become the most free nation in the world.

In this address, Jackson simultaneously conjured up a counterpublic, an underdog, on whose side he stood, and rehearsed the slogan of deliberative democracy built on a free press. Explicitly presenting the colonial ruler as a role model to which the island should aspire, Jackson also claimed a political desire in agon to the colonial administration. Jackson continued with a call for civil and 'inalienable' rights to the downtrodden and with the hope that the newspaper can 'promote a better feeling between the two factions, and hope finally to create a United Santa Cruz, and *a new people*, bonded in love and union' (31.10.15; my emphasis). Although Jackson was surely aware of the precarious legal status of the subjects of St. Croix, he nevertheless pursued an argument for civil rights and justice through a free press. However, it is important to note that Jackson made these cries for civil rights as a citizen himself. It was his insistence that he belonged to a particular community and political project, in a time and place that blurred the boundaries of professional and citizen journalism and of national imaginaries, that *The Herald* may be perceived as citizen journalism. I follow this line of thought, which allows for a redefinition of citizen journalism.

THE DE- AND RETERRITORIALIZATION OF 'THE PEOPLE'

There is a distinct development throughout the issues of *The Herald* from activist political and defiant call for citizenship, explicitly seeking to change the island and labourers' conditions, to a more subdued style of writing during the early US era, from 1917 to 1925. These developments may be characterised as territorializations of the definitions and practices of citizens. In the late era, the overt socialism and explicit calls for social reform are replaced by praise for an abstract notion of freedom and democracy, while Jackson simultaneously but indirectly shed light on the stifling and perhaps even politically paralysing events of the ongoing World War I and the racial tensions and lynchings taking place in the US South (17.7.17; 3.8.17). But by 1920, when citizenship for islanders was yet again on the table,[4] Jackson seemed to rediscover his hope for Americanism: He wrote enthusiastically about the role of African Americans in US society (23.9.20), argued for the Americanness of universal suffrage (15.11.20) and saluted the right to vote for president, which had not yet been granted to islanders.[5]

These movements shift the groundings of 'the People' Jackson addresses. Whereas the years under Danish rule deterritorialized the position of the islands' African Caribbean labourers, Americanism seemed to represent a reterritorialization: a new normal of which the Crucians might become a part. The first years of *The Herald* were filled with phrases like 'the people's press', 'social reform' and 'comrades', culminating in the slogan reiterated by Jackson in his editorials as well as by his colleagues in their opinion pieces: 'Give us the reform, or sell' (cf. 27.7.16; 31.7.16). But the post-transfer *Herald* (despite intermittent enthusiastic outbursts) recited the Declaration of Independence (3.7.17);[6] analysed the legal differences between citizens, nationals and subjects (17.2.19); and finally – after the congressional committee that was hoped to bring the future and the immense democracy of the United States to the islands failed to recommend US citizenship for their inhabitants – ended up referring to the US transfer as the 'early period of *American occupation* of these islands' (11.4.22; my emphasis). Jackson went so far as to admit to the strained relationship in which the press found itself during the war: 'Here, the threats we have received from high officials have made us to come to the conclusion that it is dangerous to run a newspaper, as a newspaper ought to be run these days' (21.3.19). These are words uttered by an editor who founded the newspaper to the sound of jeers and threats of warships. The grounds were shifting anew, and a deterritorialization was coming, but this time on different terms.

Let us unpack these movements with close reference to Jackson's writings and the geopolitical workings of the day: The sale of the islands had been underway for years, yet the labour debate and eventually the strike stirred up and managed by Jackson's labour union work arguably presented the Danish government with a troublesome colonial territory with which it could not really be bothered. Earlier, prior to *The Herald*'s establishment, Denmark had begun negotiations about the future of the islands and how to introduce Danish welfare and justice to the colonies. These were the reforms for which Jackson and his peers were calling when they shouted, 'Give us reforms, or sell', and their claim to rights as citizens seemed to have been heard and possibly answered. However, when the first rumours of a pending sale began emerging a little over a week after the strike ended (14.3.16), Jackson refrained from commenting directly until the sale was nearly finalised. It was not until Washington officially notified the islanders that negotiations between Denmark and the United States were approaching completion and that the price was set at $25 million in gold (27.7.16) that Jackson ventured his somewhat vague opinion, given his previous statements on the subject. On 31 July 1916, Jackson outlined what he saw as the possibilities for the political future of the islands: sale, reform or rolling back of reforms. Jackson believed that the local Colonial Council was pursuing the latter option. Even so, 'a change in administration is inevitable. The black people don't like [Governor] Helweg-Larsen and he doesn't like them. He should be replaced or transfer is preferable' (6.7.16). Indeed, Jackson's stance in the matter seems to be that anything was preferable to the status quo in which Jackson's nemesis, Helweg-Larsen, ruled the islands. Anything was better, be it a new administration or the desired reforms under the current ruler, so long as something happened. Beneath this wish simply for a change to the status quo lay the issue of racial belonging and another history based on a different experience. In an editorial on 1 August 1916, Jackson wrote:

> We do not look for social equality, for we believe it to be detrimental to our progress as a race, and we do not assume to rule or bully any other people. All we ask is that we be granted civil rights as law abiding citizens, and that we be guaranteed protection under the law against all the outrages common to the people of St. Croix.

This rather humble way of phrasing a rights claim owed something to Booker T. Washington, the major black intellectual of the time and a person about whom Jackson had previously and extensively published articles. Booker T. Washington's approach to racial inequality focussed on African Americans' own efforts to change their circumstances rather than on the structural racism of white folks, which was the approach and perspective taken by his contemporary and editor of *The Crisis*, W. E. B. Du Bois. Both men featured prominently in the pages of *The Herald*. Perhaps Jackson's silence regarding the sale is strategic; perhaps he did not wish to speak out of turn. In any case, at least in *The Herald*, Jackson is uncharacteristically quiet on the issue of the sale. At this point in time, Jackson had been agitating for social reforms on the islands for over a year, and although the fruits of his labour were finally within reach, he seemed uncertain. Fear of change seemed to haunt him in the days leading up to the announcement, when 'feelings of belonging' (31.7.16 by Paul E. Joseph) and advice 'not to be too confident' about the future (10.8.16) were prevalent in the pages of *The Herald*.

Once the sale became a reality, however, Jackson seemed supportive. The Danish government requested that he bring them the 'people's opinion' (16.8.16), and he responded to the best of his convictions that the transfer to US jurisdiction was favoured among the islands' inhabitants.[7] Jackson gathered people for an unofficial vote and found himself overwhelmingly in the right: He reported that, in Christiansted, 2,429 voted in favour with 1 vote against, and in Frederiksted, 2,298 voted in favour with 6 votes against. These were obviously not statistically viable numbers, as half the people gathered were ineligible to vote, and some were children. Moreover, the island was inhabited by around fifteen thousand people at this time, so the group that voiced support for Jackson and the transfer made up only a third of the population. Nevertheless, since these people had been invited through Jackson and *The Herald*, we may assume that they were readers of *The Herald* and supporters of Jackson's cause. This supports the argument that Jackson had himself been in favour of the sale all along. Perhaps he had lost faith in the desired social reforms occurring within the Danish realm, and perhaps the racism of colonialism seemed insurmountable. Thus, despite his anxious words prior to the announcement, Jackson and his peers regarded the transfer as a welcome opportunity. Articles about strong feelings of belonging to Denmark (31.7.16) and humble rights claims (1.8.16) were replaced by pieces entitled 'A Glorious Future' (11.8.16 by Chas. B. Malone) and an editorial on women's opportunities under US rule (14.8.16). Both struck an almost sanguine note in their songs of reterritorializing the Crucian people under the wings of the admired Americanism.[8]

However, as it happened, the new United States Naval administration left the island in limbo between colonial and American law: The legal texts were opaque, and the practices were inconsistent.[9] This limbo pushed Jackson to address another public, encompassing a wider segment of the islands' population. Whereas Jackson had earlier spoken of 'the people', he had really meant the labourers. Now, he was speaking to and about 'Santa Cruzians', who, depending on their differentiated status before the transfer, had different interests to protect. It was difficult to bring together a diverse group of people with a common colonial and racial past, and the tensions were palpable. Jackson, however, was not giving up his position on racial inequalities in order to please the landowners and citizens. He insisted on addressing a counterpublic even though some members of the Crucian public could not be said to inhabit this position. As so often before, Jackson called for clear-headedness:

> There are a number of persons, even in higher walks of life, who seem really not to understand the real meaning of the terms 'Government' and 'People'. The thoughts

recorded by advanced thinkers relative to the subject of government of a people must therefore be a source of misunderstanding and moreso if those thoughts are expressed by a person of color. (9.4.23)

However, despite the community's support for Jackson, despite his obvious wit and intelligence and despite his political industriousness, Jackson was 'cheated out' of a seat on the Colonial Council in May 1923, and his political ambitions were slighted. He nevertheless continued his engagement by speaking at Council meetings and using *The Herald* to inform and dispute, though now in a more traditionally journalistic way. To be sure, journalistic ethics had always been a beacon for Jackson's practice and part of the universal standard to which his articles referred. Now though, the counterpublic was becoming *the* public of St. Croix. Although still in opposition to the Americans, the colonial past of slavery and exploitation that defined the Danish–St. Crucian relationship no longer made sense in the new constellation between a St. Crucian public and an American administration. *The Herald*'s racial aspects were also changing, and the paper sought to slot itself into African American history, difficult though this fit might have been (26.7.23; 24.8.23):

> Our condition is not as bad as theirs by far, but it is wretched enough.... We would be glad to receive contributions from the pen of the citizens, for it is THE PEOPLE who rule in any democratic country. (24.8.23)

As this brief review of *The Herald*'s ten years of publication has shown, the 'heres' and 'theres' of cosmopolitan connections and of citizenship claims were shifting under Jackson's feet: Those with whom St. Croix could politically relate and engage transitioned from Danish progressives to New York civil rights activists, Crucians and, at times, other Caribbean island communities. Clearly, the idea of citizenship, of a public and of a people moved across different stages throughout the printed life of *The Herald*. These stages were indicative of both major world political developments and Jackson's personal interests, yet they drove his project of political emancipation for the islands' African Caribbean people. As I shall explore next, these movements of de- and reterritorializations can be identified in the shifting relationships between the political and citizenship.

THE TELEGRAPH AND OBJECTIVE COSMOPOLITANISM

The relations at stake in *The Herald* at the time were far from purely local. Indeed, the 'new people' to whom Jackson referred in the early editions arguably encompass a cosmopolitan community. Obviously, the colonial presence was crucial to global relationships, but other relationships were important in the (post)colonial newspaper's journalistic and cultural practices as well. I will turn to these next in a discussion of how Jackson's and *The Herald*'s political act connected the world in a cosmopolitan fashion without fully reproducing or creating the performative and colonial public of objective and technologically enhanced journalism – that is, the idea of journalism and its perceived interrelatedness with cosmopolitan sensibilities. This relational approach allows for agonistic tension.

If *The Herald*'s establishment and the newspaper's contents were of a globally connective and cosmopolitan quality, it may partly be because the world at the turn of the twentieth century was already becoming smaller and more accessible. It is often noted that transport and communication were necessarily connected up until the introduction of the telegraph, when physical travel was no longer needed to spread news (cf. Carey 1992; Rantanen 2003, 2007). However, although *The Herald* featured news from the wire, bringing despatches from World War I, Jackson built a transnational public for and with the African Caribbean labourers in St. Croix through a far more grounded and embodied practice. Rather than filling the pages with global news coming over the wire, he connected the populations of St. Croix, St. Thomas and St. John with the contemporary African American political culture in New York as well as the Danish progressive movement by sharing social and political ideologies and references to political events in local journals. In the following, I argue that by addressing a relational, political public rather than *the* public, *The Herald* would and could not rely upon professional, objective journalistic practice, which was slowly gaining ground in the early twentieth-century United States.

By 1915, when Jackson established *The Herald* in St. Croix, journalism as a professional practice was developing notions of journalistic 'objectivity', mainly in the United States, through new study programmes at major universities and through the technology of the wire. Journalism's ability to reach far beyond the borders of the nation-state without the aid of physical transport was first achieved through the telegraph (Carey 1992, Stephens 1988). The cost of sending and receiving news through this novel technology was based on the number of words used in the report, resulting in shorter and to-the-point reports. Moreover, the telegraph companies sold the news to a variety of outlets, meaning that they had to be politically neutral so as not to leave out potential buyers who subscribed to particular political views. Scholars of journalism have used both these implications of the introduction of the telegraph for communication in general and journalism in particular to argue that the wire helped create the familiar journalistic style of writing objective and factual news (Carey 1992; Schudson 1978, 2003; Schudson and Anderson 2009). Carey (210), for instance, argues that in terms of language, the telegraph demanded '"scientific" language, a language of strict denotation'. This led to a standardised language that would be understood in the same manner everywhere as an invisible way of spreading 'God's word' and enabling equality and sameness to all people (206–9). 'The origins of objectivity may be sought therefore in the necessity of stretching language in space. . . . [T]he telegraph changed the forms of social relations mediated by language' (210).

In turn, arguments such as Carey's helped support the myth of neutral technology. The global reach and connectivity of technologically enabled journalism, along with its focus on objectivity, underlined the professionalised practice as a marker of equal value among peoples. That is, if all spoke the same universal (God's word), technologically amplified language, then no word or people would be above another, and truth would naturally follow. Furthermore, global technology enabled the attribution of cosmopolitan potential to journalistic practice because the standardised, universal language could spread around the world, uncontaminated by human culture, religion and politics. Journalism's traditional focus on objectivity, and consequently on truth and impartiality, thus allows journalism to understand itself as a potentially cosmopolitan practice par excellence, embodying cosmopolitanism's values of universal solidarity, equality and justice (see Ward 2008; see also Braidotti et al. 2013, Haraway 1988).

Despite Jackson's enthusiasm and belief in journalism's abilities, already in light of 1915, this picture of universalising and cosmopolitan technology – in this case, the telegraph – may be contested. In the United States, the technology of the telegraph was controlled by the white majority and favoured commercially viable news, thereby homogenizing the news flow (Gonzáles and Torres 2011). Printing had become cheaper and circulation widespread, and although there was keen interest in portraying the social inequalities in society both in the United States and in Denmark, journalists specialising in this 'beat' – the so-called muckrakers – focussed exclusively on poor white people. This development 'effectively curtailed any hope for structured change in the nation's mass media at the dawn of the twentieth century', argue Gonzáles and Torres (182). Moreover, the neutral manner of encompassing all within the realm of sameness using technology's claim to objectivity brought with it 'a change in the actual content and style of news reporting, so that racial stereotyping and the white racial narrative became systemic and widespread in American journalism' (137). Short and to-the-point reports favoured headlines over in-depth background journalism. Stereotypes were more easily digestible to American readers, and at times the reports even instigated violence against minorities by advancing racial stereotypes under the guise of objectivity, as Gonzáles and Torres (2011) show in their comprehensive study of the minority press in the United States. Rather than connecting and universalising God's word (Carey 1992), the telegraph and the subsequent centralisation of news became a backdrop for the portrayal of race relations and reintroduced class stratifications between people who had access to news and information and people who did not. Rather than a universal moral and cosmopolitan connectivity, then, the telegraph and objectivity contributed to the ignoring of minority communities, creativity and citizens' voices.

If the use of the concept of objectivity and the cosmopolitan argument for universal solidarity seem flawed, it is not only because journalism's main and universal tenet – cosmopolitanism through objectivity – cannot help but be supported by particularities of eras, beliefs and judgements of fairness (Ward 2008; see also Braidotti et al. 2013, Haraway 1988), such as those of the muckrakers and their journalistic peers. It is also because objectivity can be said to do the exact opposite of connecting discrete world communities and enabling solidarity. Instead, the dominance of Westernised standards, eras and beliefs is implicit in the representation of journalism history and theory, and this dominance effectively excludes a variety of voices and community representations from the mediated public debate, then as now. Perhaps tellingly, Jackson mainly used the wire to report on news from the World War I frontlines and only in short despatch news. Looking for cosmopolitan connections and citizens' journalism involves consideration of the political and embodied engagements of subjects struggling to gain rights and political voice through publication. I will back up this claim in the final segment with examples from *The Herald* and Jackson's journalistic practices.

EMBODIED COSMOPOLITANISM

Because the epistemological and ontological arguments for an objective journalistic practice are contestable, journalistic objectivity is often approached as a practice (Boudana 2011, Ward 2008). However, the nature of journalism makes it a practice that simultaneously produces and addresses its public – that is, a performative practice. In the terminology of Isin (2002; see also Isin and Nielsen 2008) and as argued in chapter 2, journalism is a performative act that calls communities into existence on a global scale through the particular frames and narratives guiding journalistic as well as citizen media reporting (Chouliaraki 2013b). Because media technologies and platforms form such a large part of our daily lives, they become structures through which we understand our political and social contexts. Journalism uses certain narratives and structures – frames – that consumers of news recognize and only through which they can comprehend news. In order to break these frames of technologically enhanced objectivity, citizen journalism must be agonistic. Narrative structure needs to be ruptured through or against journalism in order to create a (counter)public, a counter-narrative.

Arguably, at stake in today's framing of certain stories and narratives are the contemporary versions of the structures of inclusion and exclusion introduced by the telegraph and their use as foundations for claims of objectivity as solidary connectivity as discussed above. The framing favours a paradigm compatible with modern thoughts on universal freedom and rights but neglects or even silences other or othered voices and communities if they do not speak the required 'language'. Indeed, standardised and universalised language is stretched rather than diversified and potentially leaves the receiver of the mediated messages without a sense of connection or relation – the story could be told from anywhere. In order for a virtual and potentially cosmopolitan space to be convincing, the actors – journalists and communities – need to be able to interact as well as be able to experience the space. Media theorist Terhi Rantanen (2003) shares the phenomenological emphasis on the importance of experience and place. Rantanen (436) argues that rather than obliterating readers' sense of place by connecting distant corners of the world without the use of physical transport, communication builds a bridge between a distinct 'here' and a distinct 'there'. Rantanen (437) argues this by furthering the idea of phenomenological geography in which:

the fundamental difference between traditional and phenomenological geography is that the latter is about people's own experience, how they feel about places, while the former is an outsider's view that claims to be objective because it is based on maps.

Rantanen's starting point in the theory that journalism is a product of communication embedded in networks of cosmopolitan cities rather than national imaginaries helps explain her emphasis on place as pivotal to worldly connectivity, to cosmopolitanism. This notion is based on experience rather than objective distance and views from nowhere (Haraway 1988, Rosen 2008), and the places of which Rantanen speaks are experienced as communities, as personalised, and from a minority position (Rantanen 2007, 847). Importantly, they are not national. How might such a phenomenological geography be imagined? Carey (1992) reminds us that communication is a process through which humans, animals, objects and places interact through the means of symbols and signs. Moreover, communication is an act that helps create society. Since Benedict Anderson's (1991) work, the newspaper has been understood as a cultural product that creates an imaginary community through time and distribution. Time – the date on the front page – connects the eclectic events reported in the newspaper, and distribution secures a mass audience, who all receive the same reports, thereby encompassing everyone in the imaginary community (Anderson 1991, 33–35). The fact that the community is imaginary does not make it unreal. To the contrary, both Anderson and Carey argue that the communicative community is constitutive of society through ritualistic and repetitive acts of language, reading and following the news and its stories' 'characters' and 'plots'. These communities, Rantanen maintains, need not be geographically delimited but are based on affective, embodied and experienced senses of belonging. While this theory may be understood in terms of physical and geographical boundaries, I suggest that we also think of Rantanen's bridges as planes of intensities and imaginary or memorised experiences. That is, they represent a process of reworking political subjectivity through imaginative and creative practices (Braidotti 2006b). It is moreover this situated, embodied and political perspective that is often regarded as authentic, and hence truthful, in contemporary citizen journalism productions, such as mobile phone footage from natural disasters and opinion-led blogs (Blaagaard 2013). In contrast to professional and objective reporting, a redefined citizen journalism could be understood as situated and embodied, characterised by the influence of subjective imagery and storytelling (Allan and Thorsen 2009). It follows from this perspective that producers of citizen journalism speak to a differently understood public – an affective and participatory public, to which they themselves belong. This conceptualisation of citizen journalism's potential for political agency, furthermore, calls upon a differently construed idea of cosmopolitanism, which may take its starting point in phenomenological geography and imagined communities.

As such, and in terms of belonging, *The Herald* may be regarded as citizen and cosmopolitan journalism of this kind. Divorced from the technological determinism and public supported by professional journalism, *The Herald* produced bridges of communication by inserting other newspapers' articles alongside local news, and their proximity on its pages became proximity in readers' minds (cf. Anderson 1991). This creation of a cosmopolitan space was a political act, yet in arguing this point, I turn to theories known for their lack of political awareness – particularly Henry Jenkins's (1992, 2006) theory of 'convergence culture' or 'textual poaching', which arguably depoliticises cultural online practices (see Fuchs 2014). Nevertheless, rather than lamenting the theories' lack of political propensity, I couple them with the previously introduced political act of citizenship and of engaging publics. Jenkins's theory of 'poaching', then, becomes an act that may be likened to Fraser's recirculation of discourse and put to political use within a certain context of political struggle for subjectivity and citizenship.

COSMOPOLITAN POACHING IN *THE HERALD*

Reading de Certeau, Jenkins (1988, 86–87) suggests that poaching is:

> a type of cultural bricolage through which readers fragment texts and reassemble the broken shards according to their own blueprint, salvaging bits and pieces of found material in making sense of their own social experience. . . . It is a way of appropriating media texts and rereading them in a fashion that serves different interests, a way of transforming mass culture into popular culture.

Jenkins uses the concept of 'poaching' to enlighten readers about fan communities' interactions with and about certain mediated texts, such as the *Star Trek* TV series. Similarly, Zizi Papacharissi (2015) argues in an introductory article to the *Social Media + Society* journal that we have always been social and that media has historically always been used to connect and to socialise. Jenkins (2009) goes further in criticising the technophilia of the YouTube generation, which focusses solely on digital interactions: If we forget the past Do-It-Yourself (DIY) video projects and fan fiction publications, Jenkins stresses, we forget the minorities of YouTube's plenitude, and we exclude the feminist and queer activism, the racial multitudes, and the anti-capitalist ideas of participatory culture that came before. Jenkins (111–13, 117) traces YouTube's current popularity back to zine culture and DIY newsrooms of the 1970s and 1980s, to cyberculture in the 1960s, and reminds us of the women's collectives' video productions of the mid-1970s, which created videos using two VCRs and patch cords. For Jenkins, it is not just a matter of using technology to engage in an already mediated community but also of creating communities through the uses of communicative media – and that, I add, may be a political act.

I use Jenkins's concept of 'poaching', understood as a means of bringing about a cultural experience of a society by appropriating generalised narratives to fit and explore a different, agonistic experience of culture and politics. I wish to suggest that, rather than using the telegraph to connect to the universalised and arguably white world of the colonisers, Jackson's *The Herald* created an agonistic bricolage constituting the cosmopolitan, colonial place of St. Croix. In line with Jackson's transnational connections, he accomplished this by selecting and publishing reading lists, including publications by W.E.B. Du Bois and Booker T. Washington, disseminating articles about the work done by these early civil rights activists and addressing cultural questions such as the importance of music. A further example is an article entitled 'Getting Together', which was reprinted from *The Outlook*, an African American journal published on the East Coast of the United States. This article presented the socialist and revolutionary vision as a moral development in which class relations and mutual hate and destruction are things of the past (13.1.16). Similarly, a reprint of an article by Ella Wheeler Wilcox from *The New York Evening Standard* explained the necessity of believing in oneself (22.1.16). As shown above, Jackson made political statements of a socialist disposition and called for the empowerment of the African Caribbean people. He underscored these statements by republishing articles from like-minded people in New York and Copenhagen. The relational networking and circulation practices of *The Herald* also reached within the community to connect and empower the colonies' labourers and citizens. For instance, *The Herald* frequently published letters to the editor, and islanders wrote articles and opinion pieces for the paper. Moreover, Jackson discussed the public's relationship with the governor, the gendarmes and the landowners, arguing against the closure of the rum shops. He argued in favour of education and social help for single mothers. On 17 January 1916, the paper published an article by a local Ralph J. Bough arguing for compassion for the poor of St. Croix, citing the empathy of Booker T. Washington as well as Abraham Lincoln and calling his insights 'a deep sense of human rights, . . . and keenly susceptible to the needs of a people' (17.1.16). Interestingly, this piece connects to the American community rather than the colonial administration. Whereas praise for Danish freedom was connected with the press and civil liberties, it seems that moral and religious solidarity was found with the United States and with African American communities.

Because of their proximity on the pages, these inputs were related to and defined through relationships with the citizens of the Virgin Islands and the global discussions of racial struggles and politics in the United States and Denmark. In this manner, *The Herald* functioned as a connection to other political cultures. By republishing articles from *The Outlook*, *The Pathfinder*, and *The Crisis*, *The Herald* connected intellectually and culturally to a progressive and burgeoning civil rights movement in New York and created a larger community in which the African Caribbean people of St. Croix could reflect their own circumstances. A colonial newspaper like *The Herald* belonged to a journalistic practice that agitated in favour of civil rights and liberties and presented arguments countering the mainstream publics in the United States and Denmark while using the rhetoric and medium of these publics. But although Jackson used a medium of mainstream deliberation, the cosmopolitanism of the paper's journalistic practices was of a different quality from the popular telegraph, as argued here. Because of its eclectic, relational and political style of 'poaching' reports from politically and culturally allied global places rather than connecting through technological and supposedly neutral wires, *The Herald* may be regarded as a cosmopolitan public. *The Herald* thus addressed and created a public situated in agon to the mainstream colonial and white US representation through a selection and collection of narratives relevant and related to the African

Caribbean subjects of the Virgin Islands and their experience and sense of belonging to a global – but not (necessarily) colonial – community.

POLITICAL CITIZEN JOURNALISM

The Herald took inspiration from progressives in Copenhagen and, most importantly, from the burgeoning civil rights movement in New York. The technologies that made this effort possible were, however, many. Alongside Jackson's editorial writings that commented on local politics and events, it was the cultural practice of poaching texts and arguments from related journals in the United States and Denmark that presented the backbone of *The Herald*'s political efforts and acts of creating a public by combining faraway places in a space of cosmopolitan proximity: the newspaper pages. These technologies and practices allowed *The Herald* to position the islands' community and the local experience within a cosmopolitan *and* colonial setting. This mode of communication was obviously journalistic (in line with the medium used) although, as a clear product of its progressive tradition, *The Herald* did not pretend to feature objective and performative reporting but instead sought to speak with a communal and educational voice, creating an agonistic position and space. From this perspective, the educational and social aspects of *The Herald* were markedly political as means of addressing and bringing into existence a caring, politicised public.

If *The Herald* was cosmopolitan, it is because it was made up of political acts, grounded in and connected to transnational ethical and political places, rather than because of universalising tendencies. Indeed, universal ideals at the time of *The Herald* were accessible only through already-privileged positions, which were then performed and reproduced. The newspaper's politics focussed on civil rights and the rights of the African Caribbean labourers – that is, agonistic politics – and the connections were transnational extensions of such localised political causes. *The Herald* was, then, a political act of cosmopolitan relation in the Danish colonies. Moreover, *The Herald* may be understood as an act of citizen journalism and cosmopolitan community building, circumventing the technological hype and journalism-centred debates about the practice. Its practice and existence may also be read as a critique of the logic of modernity in which language, race and territory define the nation-state and citizenship. *The Herald* challenged this logic by constructing a space from, of and for the embodied experience of its particular citizens across languages and territorial boundaries.

The political acts of cosmopolitanism as theorised and discussed here are moreover connected to the past in specific ways. The collective and cultural memory of enslavement was at the foundation of the political act of Jackson's labour union work as well as of *The Herald*. The inspiration drawn from New York's publicists and civil rights activists may have changed underway, yet the embodiedness of African diasporic memory and experience brings with it another cartography, one that is connected to memory and what has been termed 'The Black Atlantic' (Gilroy 1994). In my second close reading of *The Herald*, I turn to this cartography, exploring temporality's relationship to journalism.

NOTES

1. Denmark was the colonial ruler of a small area in East India; a small area of the Gold Coast in current Ghana, West Africa; the three Caribbean islands of St. Thomas, St. John and St. Croix; and in the northern colonies of Greenland, the Faroe Islands, Iceland and Norway. Of particular interest to this analysis and argument are the Caribbean possessions that, along with Fort Christiansborg in Ghana and Copenhagen in Denmark, made possible the triangular trade of enslaved people, sugar and rum between the three continents.

2. A fireburn was a form of revolt used by the enslaved people. In St. Croix, St. Thomas and St. John, three women (Queen Mary, Agnes and Mathilda) were leaders of these fireburn rebellions. A man called General Buddhoe is generally recognised as the leader of the rebellion that resulted in emancipation. In the Crucian narrative, it is General Buddhoe, rather than the Danish governor, who is credited for liberation. The discrepancy between Danish and Crucian cultural memory prompted debate in 1998, when the 150th anniversary of the emancipation was celebrated on the islands by Danish actors and brass bands (see Blaagaard 2011).

3. Jackson's writings on the strike will be analysed in depth in chapter 4.

4. The issue of the islanders' right to US citizenship when the islands were transferred to US jurisdiction was raised on several occasions from 1917 to 1925 and is arguably ongoing. See chapter 4 for a discussion of US citizenship and related political tensions.

5. The inhabitants of the US Virgin Islands are still not eligible to vote for president due to their legal status of an unincorporated territory.

6. Chapter 4 elaborates upon the mentioning and discussion of the Declaration of Independence in *The Herald*.

7. The inhabitants of the islands were not asked prior to the decision to sell, nor did they participate in the election. The implications of selling colonial possessions along with the inhabitants seems outrageous, but is rarely discussed in these terms in Denmark.

8. For Jackson, 'Americanism' is not the food Americans eat or the bootleg alcohol they drink; Americanism is the spirit of equality and democracy (11.4.22). Americanism holds the key to the prosperous future of the black communities across the United States (21.10.20). In October 1920, Jackson graduated from Howard University and proudly wrote of the multiple races that received an education there (21.10.20) as an example of American opportunities.

9. It should be noted that *The Herald* is not consistent on these issues either, publishing articles that argue for citizenship and those that say citizenship is already bestowed (cf. 17.2.19; 12.9.23).

4

Embodied Citizen Journalism

Archives and Postcolonial Memory

Referred to as 'the first draft of history', news journalism focusses on news and events that may or may not end up in the history books once time has edited the draft and selected the parts that turn out to fit a larger narrative. The relationship between journalism and history or historical narratives and memory is, however, complex. Undeniably, journalists use historical facts to understand and contextualise current events and at times show particular interest in the topic of history itself, in forms of commemoration or by drawing upon historical analogies to give a news item depth and relevance (Zelizer 2010). However, the thrust of journalism's historical implications rests on its ability to repeat and solidify the national or collective memory. Reiterations of well-known and memorable events in a nation's history as well as implicit assumptions about the national character continuously perform the collective, national belongingness and exceptionalism through journalistic mediations and technologies. Journalism by necessity tells the version of history upon which the powerful agree: the always already accepted common good and *the* public's interest.

The process of editing historical facts has already begun in the pages of the newspaper and on television screens. Nevertheless, performances and reiterations include slight changes and differences. Every repetition exists in a new context and fosters new expressions and materials. Moreover, if journalism performs certain cultural and national traits through reiteration of historical and memorable events, it may potentially be used to disrupt the collective stories by consciously telling new ones. Finally, time may have gotten the editing wrong, for instance by deleted passages that were deemed unimportant to the majority or to those in power or that emphasised points and events in order to fit an already popular narrative. Henry Jenkins (2009), in his much-cited essay on the history of the participatory culture of YouTube, states that a sense of plenitude often masks silences and absences. For instance, Western communication theory – in particular, theories regarding journalism and public communicative engagement – is dominated by a logic of deliberative publics. Such theories belong to a significant extent to the legacy of Habermas's public sphere, narratives of Western conception and the heritages of freedom of expression and citizen engagement. These narratives are performative in the sense that the narrative of deliberative journalism and the following theories are simultaneously retold, produced and hence performed – and end up producing a modern logic (Shome 2009, Goldberg 2002) of citizenship. Within this performative narrative, subjects who do not immediately fit the national self-understanding and identity or who have been displaced within the narrative, such as (post)colonial subjects, are cast in binary relation to the Western (often white and male) and colonising culture as victims in need of humanitarian help, rather than as citizens possessing communicative agency (Chouliaraki 2013b). This logic, as discussed in the previous chapters, leads to an understanding of deliberative engagement and citizenship as always already Western and modern. Furthermore, this logic and its implications are mirrored in the postcolonial West's diverse, mediated debates about race and migrants because these reproduce a power relation based on the power to define and take ownership of Western paradigms and their concomitant societies.

Many silences and absences in the theory of journalism stem from the colonial history of the very notion of 'freedom of expression' and of the idea of citizens' engagement through journalism. Not unexpectedly, as in the case of the minority press in the United States, colonial history goes unmentioned in most journalistic history, as the silencing of this historical fact and its political implications for postcolonial Europe and the United States is part and parcel of the logic of modernity (Shome and Hegde 2002, Spivak 1988). The history of journalism produced in the field is indeed presented as the history of Anglo-American and European mainstream press, as is evident in numerous books on the topic (e.g., Allan 2012, Peters and Broersma 2013, Starr 2004, Stephens 1988; see also the critique by Gonzáles and Torres 2011). This history, of course, encompasses participatory forms of journalism, as discussed in chapter 2. Moreover, as Shome (2009) and Shome and Hegde (2002) note, there are also postcolonial readings of media and journalism, which often, however, focus on the politics of representation and the spectres of the colonial past in present-day journalism and popular culture.[1] Rather than focussing on the politics of representation of (post)colonial subjects, in this chapter I continue to read *The Herald*, produced by and for the African Caribbean population in the Danish colony of St. Croix, as a political production of citizenship. *The Herald* is a historical case, an archived newspaper, and therefore a documented cultural history. As a practice of not only resistance against the universalising concept of individual rights and freedoms but also a rights claim and a struggle to gain voice and presence in the history books, *The Herald* tells a different story of the history of journalism, the history of Danish colonialism and the history of United States citizenship and racial politics. By focussing on the particular, grounded case of *The Herald*, I question the Western history of journalism and its relationship to citizenship as well as critique the claim of universality of individual rights and freedoms.

In chapter 3, I read *The Herald* as a production of citizenship – a technology of the African Caribbean population on St. Croix – that shifts and pushes boundaries of identification and knowledge as the political geography changes around the postcolonial press and population. These practices and acts of citizenship, I argued, are movements of de- and reterritorializations of citizenship in a particular postcolonial context. This approach allows me to support my argument that *The Herald* is an instance of citizen journalism, defined as such by the rights claims, political acts, and transformations that citizen journalism fosters. In this chapter, I focus on time as I trace shifting positions actively using history and memory – mnemonic processes – that Jackson creates throughout his work as editor of *The Herald*. Movements of archiving, archaeological knowledge productions and genealogy continue to reveal new perspectives and understandings of citizenship – and citizen journalism – on the islands. This point requires some elaboration, and I therefore begin by placing *The Herald* in the present, in the material archives, before engaging in a close reading of two particularly defining editorials authored by Jackson that raise questions with regard to the performing of memory. These two editorials function as mnemonic snapshots, connecting readers to the past in an almost visceral way, while simultaneously pointing towards potential future political identifications. Mirroring the past and the present, Jackson references in these editorials a common memory by means of historical documents, through which the particularity of the counterpublic is made explicit and embodied.

The two events to which I pay particular attention occurred in the early days of the publication of *The Herald* and the work of the Labour Union. The first event on which I focus is the labour strike orchestrated by the Labour Union under Jackson's guidance. The second is the first Fourth of July celebrations on the islands following the transfer to US jurisdiction in 1917. These two events – understood as incorporeal transformations brought about through illocutionary speech acts in two editorials authored by Jackson – are similar in structure: Both draw upon and reprint historical documents to underscore a point about relationships to and the meaning of the past, and both editorials focus on equality and political and civil rights. However, while the similarities testify to the coherency of Jackson's political aims, the supporting historical documents demonstrate a change in embodied and situated relation to the rights claims being made. Memory and historical facts and documents underscored and sustained Jackson's cause, and the practice of poaching, reprinting and circulating historical documents on a temporal level in particular allowed *The Herald* to conjure up a public that was not only grounded and situated in the African Caribbean experience of the island of St. Croix but that was also cosmopolitan in reach and scope. While chapter 3 focussed on *The Herald*'s referencing of geographically dispersed contexts, creating bridges within a cosmopolitan counterpublic, this chapter explores a temporal referencing.

Jackson reprinted both historical and contemporary texts in *The Herald*. Over the years, this amounted to a great many republished and translated articles from around the world, though mainly from New York and Copenhagen. As discussed above, New York and Copenhagen anchored Jackson's political socialist desire for social reform. The practice of reprinting is what Rothberg (2009, 212) calls an 'orientation towards a public'. Rothberg relies on Warner's conceptualisation of a public, and his analysis centres on the literary work of the Holocaust writer Charlotte Delbo. Despite the differences in historical focus, the practices of Delbo and Jackson are related: By reproducing a particular collection of articles from Denmark and the United States, Jackson's intertextual and interdiscursive practice conjures up a reflexive public; not only a local public of actual readers but also a public connected through the circulation of thoughts and texts crossing national borders. The reflections and thoughts that these texts represent run along the lines of race and labour issues and an ambition to create and support social reform, as discussed in chapter 3. Jackson's writing thus comprises a complex web of cultural-historical, documentary and archival colonial history through means of the press.

ARCHIVES, GENEALOGIES AND MEMORY

Nearly a hundred years since the last issue of *The Herald* was sent to print, the back issues are available on microfilm, archived and stored in Denmark. As is well known, the politics of the archive contain their own imperfections and challenges. Archives are commonly understood as a collection of documents that simultaneously stabilises and produces collective memory. Denmark is famously rigorous when it comes to colonial record keeping, which has resulted in archives and projects being digitalised and made available to people who may be looking for their ancestry or are generally interested in the colonial history of the US Virgin Islands.[2] With regard to Danish colonial history, the majority of documents have previously only been stored in the Danish National Archive (Rigsarkivet) in Copenhagen and in the National Archive in Washington, D.C. Only a tiny fraction has been available to locals of and visitors to St. Croix, St. Thomas and St. John. This has led to local history being based on storytelling and cultural commemoration practices, but it has also led to resentment and calls for returning the recorded history to the islands (Bastian 2003, Blaagaard 2011). The emphasis on bringing home artefacts and materials of the past seems to grant particular currency to documentation and artefactual archives as opposed to oral history and commemorations. Although documents are now available online, issues of language, technological advancements and geography may still play a role in the politics of the archive: Who has access to and the possibility of questioning History (intentionally spelled with a capital *H* to underscore the solidity and factual nature of its narrative)? *The Herald* has only recently been digitalised and is now partly available online to subscribers and enrolled students of the universities in Denmark. It is on microfilm in the National Library in the Danish city of Aarhus, where it may be read on an analogue microfilm projector. Although the library has been known to send the film rolls out of the country to interested library loaners, it is necessary to know that the archives and microfilms exist in order to acquire them and to understand their importance. In selected excerpts, *The Herald* is on the high school curriculum for students on St. Croix, yet Crucian historians and interested residents have long been unable to peruse *The Herald* at leisure, to read the words of Jackson, a major political figure and agitator for islanders' rights[3] and for social reforms.

In light of *The Herald*'s importance to its generation of inhabitants on St. Croix and particularly to the island's labourers, its limited access today is astonishing. *The Herald* was the amplifier of Jackson's politics and efforts to bring social reform and better working conditions to the islands. Its offices were at times the home of the Labour Union's meetings, and during the labour strike and lockout shortly after the first issue of the paper had hit the streets, *The Herald* was the bulletin board for information on the ongoing strike and on how to relate to the actions taken by planters and politicians. Few articles have been written on Jackson's union activities: His work as a political agitator and his use of the press and journalism to consciously disrupt the islands' political and cultural narratives have largely been ignored in Danish academia and dismissed by Danish politicians and historians as pure rebellious agitation. Indeed, the picture of Jackson as leader of a pending rebellion that was painted by his political opponents in the colonial administration has become the standard Danish manner of narrating Jackson, if he is mentioned at all.[4] Not so in St. Croix. Building upon cultural memory, commemoration events, public spaces and artwork, Jackson's activities are well known and appreciated, even if the paper itself remains largely unread. Jackson – as both a man and a political agitator – nevertheless remains a divisive and provocative figure, including on the islands. The fact that Crucian commemoration and remembrance is stronger than that in Denmark, despite primarily Danish access to the archives, supports the argument that it is neither the documents nor memory on their own that are significant to historical knowledge but instead a combination of both. Jackson's own references to historical documents, when successful, likewise draw upon a combination of both documentation and collective, inherited memory.

The Herald and Jackson's work both document archival knowledge and produce myth and cultural memory. In other words, the archive of *The Herald* represents the ordering and editing of the colonial past *and* that original past event and memory. It is, following Derrida (1996, 17), hypomnesic: a politicised structuring and production of the past that inevitably reaches into the future and limits what may be said and thought:

> [T]he technical structure of the *archiving* also determines the structure of the *archivable* content even in its very coming into existence and in its relationship to the future. The archivization produces as much as it records the event. This is also our political experience of the so-called news media.

Using Derrida's terminology, *The Herald* may be regarded as a double-archivization. On the one hand, *The Herald* archived the process of political citizenship in the last years of Danish jurisdiction and the first years of American jurisdiction. Jackson's own reports, analysed in chapter 3, on the reception and importance of *The Herald* as a paper of the people show as much. Moreover, his use of historical documents undergirded his political points about the present and future of the islands' African Caribbean people. On the other hand, the microfilms, with their limited accessibility, have had a stifling effect on the archivization of the postcolonial, political relationship between Denmark, the United States and St. Croix. The archival process described by Derrida above impresses itself on the future and on the cultural memory by making the *records* available (or not); by leaving *traces*, ideas or notions; and by marking and *inscribing* history onto the bodies, buildings and landscapes of the inflicted culture. This is why it has consequences for how history and historical narrative are enabled and for which voices may be heard when archives are unavailable to the people and cultures they pertain to: Who is considered worth listening to? Jackson's reiterations of historical documents may also have served the purpose of performing a relationship to a past while the experiences from that past were lost. However, re-membering – bringing the historical counter-narrative into being through memory (Gilroy 2004, Braidotti 2006b) – creates the possibility of redefining our relationship to the past as well as the present. Below, I use the theories and critical assessment of memory by Gilroy and Braidotti to help me understand the political act of Jackson's editorials on two occasions as a mnemonic device. I consider the extent to which the selected editorials from *The Herald* may be understood as cultural products that through mnemonic processes create what Gilroy (2004) calls a 'changing same'. I use cartographic reading to identify whether the editorials produce an affirmative and generative political project (Braidotti 2006b).

For Derrida, the archivization process leads to melancholia and reminiscence: Archives are distinct from archaeology, which leaves the former in a tension, *aporia*, with the latter being akin to *jouissance* and creativity. I do not follow Derrida's sombre reading of the archive but instead insist on the creative relationship between the archive and archaeology. Archivization may be seen as a technology of the self (Foucault 1982) and of subjectivity concerning the connection between the subject's production of self and her affective and political interconnections in the world. Discarding the assertion that the dictum 'Know yourself' should be a question of identity, Foucault argues that the saying implies a process of subjectivity through various techniques of examining the self in a process of defamiliarization in order to apply the self to society, as a citizen. Foucault believes that the difference between this process and psychoanalytical self-examination lies in their relations to the surrounding world. Rather than focussing on insights, it is an '[a]ccounting backwards for the affective impact of various items or data upon oneself [that] is the process of remembering' (Braidotti 2006b, 173).

While *The Herald* itself is an archivization process, I argue that, given its status as a microfilm archive that has been hidden or forgotten for many years, a cartographic re-reading of such recently excavated material enables a process of memory and historical development in our contemporary understanding of colonial history and journalism. My reading produces a revival of *The Herald*'s technologies of colonial, political citizenship. That is, rather than being a static document, the newspaper's state of tension between archive, political process and narrative produced and potentially still produces what amounts to a technology of memory regarding race and class struggles in colonial St. Croix. This is a technology of the collective, postcolonial self. *The Herald* serves as a witness to the times in which it was published and to the political hopes and frustrations that simmered and occasionally boiled over into strikes and protests in the early twentieth-century Virgin Islands. Such a witness is not merely a statement or an expression; it is also a movement between past and present, among peoples and societies. It is a 'remnant' (Agamben 2002, 159), 'trace' (Derrida 1996, 25) and 'whispers of the archive' (Bastian 2003, 2). Anthropologists Olwig (1993) and Bastian consider these whispers capable of speaking the lives of the subaltern – the voice of the subaltern, those whose history is not spelled with a capital *H*, who fall between the cracks – rendering them audible to the researcher. A more philosophical approach argues that 'the truth', historical fact, lies between what is sayable and what is unsayable, the said and the unsaid (Agamben 2002, 34). If archives are witnesses, then my discursive and cartographic reading of *The Herald* is multidirectional in scope. It does not pretend to bring forth a new history or narrative of the islands. Journalism, including the kind conducted in *The Herald*, in this sense remains a first draft of history. Its reports do not constitute facts. My reading is instead one of the political intentions and hopes, the acts and performances, produced in *The Herald* and will point towards contingencies as well as breaks and inconsistencies in colonial narrative and voices – de- and reterritorializations – in order to demonstrate how *The Herald* produced embodied citizen journalism.

Developing my argument, I begin in the 'Counter-Memories' section by returning to two previously discussed scholars of postcolonial and Deleuzian thinking, Paul Gilroy and Rosi Braidotti, in order to create the cartography of memory in *The Herald* through their approach to temporality, which elaborates upon and nuances the concept of archivization. Their theorisations create the implicit underpinnings for my close readings of the editorials on the labour strike and the Declaration of Independence. Following these two analyses, the 'What is a US Citizen?' section narrates Jackson's struggle with citizenship, the public sphere and lack of political and public power following the transfer to the United States. I conclude in the 'Memories of a Shared History' section by arguing that Jackson's two editorials respectively communicated and affected an active, political response due to its embodied memory and failed to bring about a political act because of the abstract and detached structure of the memory involved. Memory, then, is a powerful generator of subjectivity, but in order for political rights claims – citizen journalistic products – to arise, memory must be employed in the service of and for an embodied community.

COUNTER-MEMORIES

Gilroy and Braidotti connect the poststructuralist and feminist critique of modernity to the embodied (sexualised, racialised, naturalised) experience of subjectivity. The dichotomous structure that Braidotti and Gilroy argue is foundational to Western philosophy and modernity needs to be deconstructed in order to give way to a counter-memory that potentially produces a counterculture and that may help combat racism and sexism. In one of his most acclaimed books, *The Black Atlantic*, Gilroy (1993, 45) understands the argument he makes in the book 'as complementing and extending the work of feminist philosophers who have opposed the figuration of woman as a sign for the repressed or irrational other of rationality identified as male'. Similar to Braidotti's (1991, 193) 'icons of the feminine', 'the icon of the blacks' (Gilroy 1993, 45) is either presented as irrational or as pure, uncorrupted nature within Western, modern philosophy. Countering these labels, Braidotti and Gilroy argue that by creatively producing counter-memories, archivization can represent a political and affirmative act that produces subjectivity formations and social change.

This is partly because Braidotti and Gilroy see subjectivity and memory as connected to the body and embodied experience. Already in her early work, Braidotti (1991, 2) identifies the French poststructuralists as basing the act of philosophy on 'the decline of reason as an ideal', which brings the crisis of rationality in Western thought to bear on the issue of subjectivity itself. This philosophical starting point – which accounts for the tension within and the necessity of deconstructing the meaning-making and politics of rationality in philosophical thought – allows Braidotti (3), following Deleuze and feminist thinking, to rethink philosophy as a '"problematic" model [that is] a political gesture, which connects the act of reflection to the context which engendered it' – that is, the embodied context matters and becomes the ground on which concepts develop. This is both a rejection of universalism and a means of questioning the corporeality of thinking, which emerged as critical counter-history in Western philosophy through feminist critique. In other words, in feminist thinking, philosophy is embodied and embedded, with the result that the particularities of experiences, bodies (female and black) and their differences matter. This is not an argument for essentialist thinking. Instead, Braidotti's rhizomatic and nomadic thinking argues for quite the opposite of essentialism when she emphasises the particularity of locations and embodiments as well as their transpositions and transformations in time and space. The importance of counter-memories and critique identified by both Gilroy and Braidotti cannot be adequately described through a call for terms such as hybridity or creolisation, if these terms assume a combination of two or more pure essences.[5] What is needed is a 'rhizomorphic, fractal structure of the transcultural, international formation' (Gilroy 1993, 4).

In chapter 1, laying out the groundwork for this book, I used the strategies of politics of location to emphasise rhizomatic thought. For Braidotti, the relationship between modernity and counter-subject formations is always already a crucial political process of archivization or a technology of the self, induced by a visceral, embodied context. Gilroy's 'Black Atlantic' is an assemblage of deterritorializations and reterritorializations, antithetical to nationalistic focus and to the traditional idea of modernity due to their processes of continuous uprooting and re-rooting, which dissuade teleological thinking and methodological nationalism. This rhizomatic manner of thinking allows Gilroy to critique Africanist essentialism and European nationalisms as well as lays the foundations for Braidotti's critical thinking about femininity and embodiment. It aims to both challenge the dominant vision of what counts as the subject of knowledge and to bring about multiple new perspectives, reflecting different life experiences (Braidotti 1994). Braidotti's and Gilroy's dream of social and political change in Europe drive them to re-engage with European historicity and memory through re-readings of their (relationships to) 'others' rather than delinking thought from the tradition of European philosophy. In other words, both Gilroy and Braidotti develop strategies for dismantling the white, male construction of knowledge and through it the accepted idea of teleological time and modern thought. They do so through critical reflections on the constitutional role played by the sexualized, racialized, and naturalised 'others' of the hegemonic Western subject. They are therefore well suited to guide critical reading of postcolonial memory.

The Changing Same

Taking the positions of the two scholars in turn: Perhaps due to its provocative stance on Africanist and pan-African movements arguing for the return to an original, authentic African philosophy, Gilroy's *Black Atlantic* was subject to much debate upon its publication (cf. Evans 2009, Winant et al. 1994). The concept encompasses both a geopolitical space and deconstruction of modernity – that is, the idea of teleologically progressive time. While Gilroy (1993, 191) spends most of the book discussing the spatiality of the Atlantic diaspora, the criss-crossing and intersecting movements of identities, ideas and ideologies, in the final chapter he turns his attention to temporality: '[the] historicity, memory or narrativity that are the articulating principles that grew inside modernity in a distinctive relationship of antagonistic indebtedness'. His conception of historicity and memory stand in opposition to the role of tradition and authenticity evoked by pan-African theorists, whose ideals bypass Western influences. As far as the present chapter is concerned, there are two significant aspects to Gilroy's focus on memory as producing counterculture. First, Gilroy reworks the idea of tradition by critiquing the removal of the memory of slavery and of European modernity – that is, the Black Atlantic – by the pan-Africanists. Second, he uses this critique to analyse expressive culture as acts of memory that simultaneously call a counterculture into being.

Gilroy (1993, 198) redefines 'tradition' as 'the living memory of the changing same'. He uses 'the changing same' to question the idea of the 'original' and of 'origin'. Memory and lived culture are always already producing and reproducing themselves, reworking what it means to say that something is original or authentic. Gilroy (198) thereby brings about an understanding of a 'non-traditional tradition', which does not stand in opposition to modernity but is instead produced through modernity and is in fact 'an irreducibly modern, ex-centric, unstable, asymmetrical, cultural ensemble'. Gilroy argues that tradition must be understood in this manner in order to rescue the concept from the 'obsession with origins' (Lott 1994, 57). He identifies this obsession in both popular and political culture, in which the Black Atlantic's many inspirational interconnections are neglected in favour of a story of purity and 'unblemished exceptionalism' (Gilroy 1993, 57). Moreover, the argument for the purity of African American tradition produces an idea of a linear time that may be rolled back to erase the horrors of enslavement as well as the mutual impact of modernity and African American culture.

In contrast with this conceptualisation of tradition, Gilroy (1993, 198) uses the example of music as a mnemonic device and argues that tradition as changing same is practiced in music and in the culture that surrounds the African American music scene. Both in terms of rhythm and in terms of lyrics, music calls for a counterculture – or counterpublic (Fraser 1990, Warner 2002) – of active listeners, who are engulfed in the memory-making of the present as the music draws in and draws upon historicity and social memory. As discussed in chapter 2, Fraser (1990) addresses the idea of subaltern publics as discursive circulations of knowledge production of resistance. In Gilroy's work, vernacular culture may be said to constitute such discursive circulation, producing political acts and counter-subject formations. A political counter-subjectivity is connected to an embodied past, allowing experiences to be carried down through generations. Popular culture such as music is not always political or always just play, Gilroy instead argues – drawing upon his personal experience – 'it wasn't just political, and the forms of pleasure that we took in it were things that had political consequences' (Lott 1994, 81). While Gilroy has been noted for paying insufficient attention to the political sphere (Evans 2009, King 2014), it is clear that his conceptualisation of music and other examples of expressive culture pursued in several publications (Gilroy 1987, 1994) as mnemonic and countercultural politics of vernacular culture allow activist or citizen media practices (Baker and Blaagaard 2016) to develop – that is, an affirmative political production of subjectivity. This is in line with the idea of counterpublics, which are publics that focus on the political as agonisms and productive interactions. While the idea of *counter*-memory may imply a binary opposition between constructions of memories, this is not necessarily Braidotti's or Gilroy's aim. Counter-memories are productive reiterations of past events – broadly speaking – that change the present and future understanding of self.

Memory as a Political Project

I now wish to return to Braidotti's understanding of a philosophical counter-history to modernity as always already political. This is partly because 'the implicitly political nature of the act of thinking . . . is the trademark of feminism as a discursive practice' (Braidotti 1991, 9) and partly because Braidotti (2006b, 167), following Glissant, 'stresses the deep generative powers of memory as a political project'. The generative powers of memory are active remembrance – that which returns and is remembered or repeated (168) – which supports and sustains a *becoming-minoritarian*. In short, whereas Gilroy remains largely silent on the political potential of the changing same and music as a mnemonic device, for Braidotti, political embodiedness constitutes the political as foundational for memory. Following Deleuze and Guattari (2004 [1980]), Braidotti presents her complex thinking of ethical relations through the concept of becoming-minoritarian, which in this sense represents a collective process of deterritorializing the subject and opening up spaces for the reinvention of a self.

That is, the subject is constantly in the process of becoming subject, and through active re-membering (taking apart and bringing back together) – not unlike Gilroy's critical counter-memory – the subject will be becoming-minoritarian, repositioning herself against majoritarian culture and politics.

This concept, then, is a productive means of thinking memory as well as of remaining attentive to Spivak's postcolonial critical thinking, notwithstanding her scholarly spat with poststructuralism, as discussed in chapter 1. Braidotti's concept of memory is thus linked to the destabilisation of the authority of experience or the original and to the imaginative and creative capacity for continuously reworking subjectivity. First, minoritarian memory questions the importance and authority of the original, majority discourse. Rather than citing an original piece of writing, for instance, when commenting upon it, one may work from memory, thereby actively producing new points of interrelationship. This is again a Deleuzian conceptualisation with which Braidotti agrees and that she develops by stressing the particular role of the feminine in the construction of master narratives and Western thought. If citation is discarded, and one works from memory, writing or production becomes a 'relay point between different moments in space and time' (Braidotti 2006b, 171) and thus nonlinear. Second, and concomitantly, memory becomes a process of affirmation and creativity: New connections are continually made in a mix-and-match growth. 'Memory is ongoing and forward-looking precisely because it is a singular yet complex subject that is always already in motion' (173). Memory is connected to the methodological strategy of *politics of location*, also introduced in chapter 1. It is a feminist strategy of situated knowledges (Haraway 1988) that produces an analysis grounded in the embodied, embedded and accountable subject. The concept is deeply connected to subject formation and political resistance as it is theorised by Braidotti, since it emphasises the personal as the political and the importance of collectively and publicly sharing the accounts of lived experience. Finally, Braidotti's conception of memory is linked to a post-psychoanalytic definition of memory. This definition sees memory as containing both conscious and unconscious traces of experiences, which may or may not pertain to one's individual life experiences. It then relies upon the ability of humans to creatively remember things that did not actually happen to them individually (Braidotti 2006b, 166–69).

Creative, Activist Memories

While Gilroy understands technologies of memory as expressed through vernacular culture, Braidotti sees thinking – and in particular feminist thinking – as a process of collective and transformative remembering and creating. The role of memory and the perception of time involves questioning and subverting the grand narratives of modernity by re-reading modern thinkers within a realm of the complex set of interactions related to race and gender as empirical and historical entities. Moreover, this memory of the embodied historical narrative is expressed and reiterated through vernacular and popular culture, thereby continuously reproducing and reworking the intermixtures, producing the changing same. For Braidotti, thinking is an embodied and practical tool to subvert received gender roles and identities, understanding and changing the world through transformation of subjectivity. Braidotti regards scholarly work as potentially activist. She shares the poststructuralist critique of master narratives, and her conception of memory highlights the untethered creativity and productivity of alternative ways of becoming subjects, which are accompanied by the potential for reinventing the subject – both in terms of relation and community. As mentioned above, the process of subjectivity can be identified in Derrida's concept of archivization as well, though Braidotti and Gilroy add a notion of memory as political action through cultural or philosophical products. Braidotti's and Gilroy's approaches make archivization relevant inasmuch as the emphasis is on creativity and *jouissance*.

In my close readings of *The Herald*'s editorial concerning the 1916 strike and the first Fourth of July celebration in 1917, it is possible to identify multilayered processes of remembering as methodological and embodied strategies of *politics of location*, while understanding the editorials as archived, expressive culture in their own right, producing a changing same. In these editorials, Jackson uses historical texts and embodied memory to re-member and capture, respectively. Jackson's uses of history and memory bear examination as a means of evoking heritage and collective subjectivity formation, while simultaneously challenging and changing the understanding of the collective self. The two events to which I turn next both invoke historical documents in order to identify and situate the readers and their political and social situation. These two events are not equally successful in producing political acts, which I argue is due to their differing levels of embodied memory.

STRIKE!

The first editorial I wish to discuss concerns the labour strike in the winter of 1916. The strike lasted for almost a month and was a long time coming: On 16 November 1915, Jackson announced the first meeting of the Labour Union in the pages of *The Herald* under the heading 'What is a Labor Union?' (16.11.15). This was the first organised attempt at gaining rights and opportunities for labourers on the island of St. Croix, despite previous protests and demonstrations. Jackson's interest in the islands' working people had been one of the main reasons for his trip to Denmark the year before, during which he asked the Danish government for social reforms, civil rights and a replacement for St. Croix's governor Helweg-Larsen, with whom Jackson had had several public disagreements. A month later, Jackson's colleague, Ralph de Chabert – a frequent writer for the paper – wrote an article titled 'The Situation', which begins with the statement that 'St. Croix is making history in these days. She is approaching a crisis'. The article argued that the crisis pertained to the majority of the population, the labouring people, who were poor and underfed. 'Are the people worthwhile helping?' the article asked rhetorically. This question, which in essence is a rephrasing of the question 'Who counts as human?' goes to the core of Jackson's fight for civil rights and enlists the power hierarchy embedded in colonial relations. Recognition of inequality and unfairness in the face of civil rights and declarations of independence grew stronger over the years, but at this early stage, the argument for human interrelational respect and the demand to simply be presented with the same opportunities as were white plantation owners were at the core of *The Herald*'s argument. The labourers were underpaid by the planters, and although the labourers were dependent upon their employer and the business, the businesses were likewise dependent upon the labourers, de Chabert's article argued. What was needed was a connecting figure and organisation. It was a direct call for a Union, which was heard and answered shortly thereafter (14.12.15). In the days running up to the announcement of the strike, as well as throughout and following the strike, *The Herald* republished articles from *The Outlook* (13.1.16), the *Colored American Review* (19.1.16), and other publications that reported on local unions and labour strikes. As in the case of previous and future article series in *The Herald*, the concept of the public – the group with common interests, addressed in the articles leading up to the strike – was expanded, absorbing new terrain through interdiscursivity and intertextuality.

On 24 January 1916, Jackson wrote: 'Labourers of the Union are striking for living wages to better their awful conditions – conditions which it is a scandal to support under the Danish flag' (24.1.16). The strike went on for over three weeks, weakening the labourers physically and the plantation owners economically. During the strike, which to this date remains one of the major labour union accomplishments on Danish soil, *The Herald* published articles that repeated the mantra of interpersonal and reciprocal respect. This sentiment was supported by none other than John D. Rockefeller Jr., who in an interview reprinted from the *New York Sunday American* (1.2.16) argued that bitterness could be avoided if people regarded one another as human beings of flesh and blood, with desires and aspirations. But as the strike ended, Jackson was asked by friends why he had 'conducted such a hot campaign against the planters [plantation owners]' (8.3.16), and his reply, which he stated in an editorial and an accompanying column, was striking both in terms of its content and form, which included a reprint of a historical text. Jackson said:

> The conduct of the planters today is very near the same as it used to be in 1783, when they had laws (see next column) to support them in their barbarous and cruel treatment of the slaves. . . . [T]here can be no difficulty in arriving at the necessity for such a hot campaign, appealing having proved fruitless. . . .
>
> A certain writer said a few days ago that a lash of abuse is sure to leave its mark behind. Yes, the lash, not alone of abuse but from the whip of the slave-owner has left the mark behind and the planter will bear it to their grave. Figuratively, then for every red-hot-iron pinch afflicted upon the bound slave, the planter shall be pinched back threefold; for every leg lost, both legs will go; for every burn in the forehead, there shall be a scalp taken; for every hundred stripes there shall be two hundred; for one case of hanging there shall be two; for every one slave branded, there shall be ten sons of slave-holders branded. Think of the things more horrible, of the slave 'pens', then think of the origin of mulattos, and you will get a clear idea of why the campaign had to be hot.

Alongside this roar of indignation, under the heading 'Laws Used for Regulating the Conduct of Slaves', were detailed eighteen kinds of corporeal punishment used

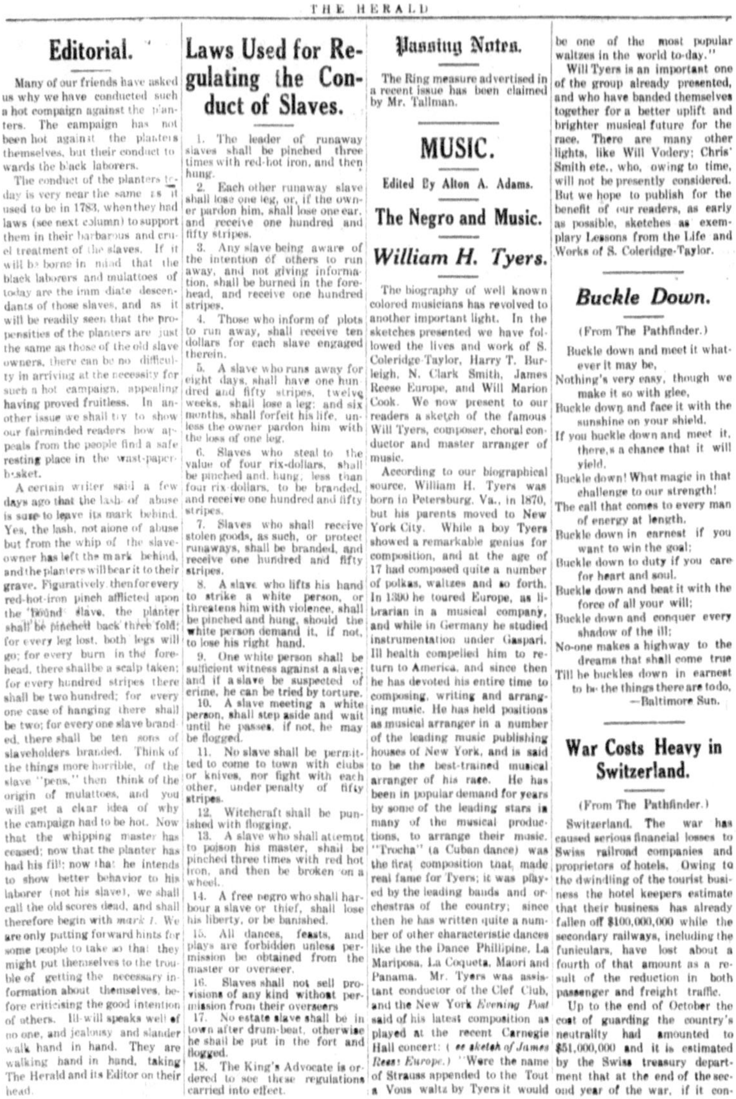

THE HERALD

Editorial.

Many of our friends have asked us why we have conducted such a hot compaign against the planters. The campaign has not been hot against the planters themselves, but their conduct towards the black laborers.

The conduct of the planters today is very near the same as it used to be in 1783, when they had laws (see next column) to support them in their barbarous and cruel treatment of the slaves. If it will be borne in mind that the black laborers and mulattoes of today are the immediate descendants of those slaves, and as it will be readily seen that the propensities of the planters are just the same as those of the old slave owners, there can be no difficulty in arriving at the necessity for such a hot campaign, appealing having proved fruitless. In another issue we shall try to show our fairminded readers how appeals from the people find a safe resting place in the wast-paper basket.

A certain writer said a few days ago that the lash of abuse is sure to leave its mark behind. Yes, the lash, not alone of abuse but from the whip of the slaveowner has left the mark behind, and the planters will bear it to their grave. Figuratively then for every red-hot-iron pinch afflicted upon the 'bound' slave, the planter shall be pinched back three fold; for every leg lost, both legs will go; for every burn in the forehead, there shall be a scalp taken; for every hundred stripes there shall be two hundred; for every one case of hanging there shall be two; for every one slave branded, there shall be ten sons of slaveholders branded. Think of the things more horrible, of the slave "pens," then think of the origin of mulattoes, and you will get a clear idea of why the campaign had to be hot. Now that the whipping master has ceased; now that the planter has had his fill; now that he intends to show better behavior to his laborer (not his slave), we shall call the old scores dead, and shall therefore begin with *mark 1*. We are only putting forward hints for some people to take so that they might put themselves to the trouble of getting the necessary information about themselves, before criticising the good intention of others. Ill-will speaks well of no one, and jealousy and slander walk hand in hand. They are walking hand in hand, taking The Herald and its Editor on their head.

Laws Used for Regulating the Conduct of Slaves.

1. The leader of runaway slaves shall be pinched three times with red-hot iron, and then hung.

2. Each other runaway slave shall lose one leg, or, if the owner pardon him, shall lose one ear, and receive one hundred and fifty stripes.

3. Any slave being aware of the intention of others to run away, and not giving information, shall be burned in the forehead, and receive one hundred stripes.

4. Those who inform of plots to run away, shall receive ten dollars for each slave engaged therein.

5. A slave who runs away for eight days, shall have one hundred and fifty stripes, twelve weeks, shall lose a leg: and six months, shall forfeit his life, unless the owner pardon him with the loss of one leg.

6. Slaves who steal to the value of four rix-dollars, shall be pinched and hung; less than four rix-dollars, to be branded, and receive one hundred and fifty stripes.

7. Slaves who shall receive stolen goods, as such, or protect runaways, shall be branded, and receive one hundred and fifty stripes.

8. A slave who lifts his hand to strike a white person, or threatens him with violence, shall be pinched and hung, should the white person demand it, if not, to lose his right hand.

9. One white person shall be sufficient witness against a slave; and if a slave be suspected of crime, he can be tried by torture.

10. A slave meeting a white person, shall step aside and wait until he passes, if not, he may be flogged.

11. No slave shall be permitted to come to town with clubs or knives, nor fight with each other, under penalty of fifty stripes.

12. Witchcraft shall be punished with flogging.

13. A slave who shall attempt to poison his master, shall be pinched three times with red hot iron, and then be broken on a wheel.

14. A free negro who shall harbour a slave or thief, shall lose his liberty, or be banished.

15. All dances, feasts, and plays are forbidden unless permission be obtained from the master or overseer.

16. Slaves shall not sell provisions of any kind without permission from their overseers

17. No estate slave shall be in town after drum-beat, otherwise he shall be put in the fort and flogged.

18. The King's Advocate is ordered to see these regulations carried into effect.

Passing Notes.

The Ring measure advertised in a recent issue has been claimed by Mr. Tallman.

MUSIC.

Edited By Alton A. Adams.

The Negro and Music.

William H. Tyers.

The biography of well known colored musicians has revolved to another important light. In the sketches presented we have followed the lives and work of S. Coleridge-Taylor, Harry T. Burleigh, N. Clark Smith, James Reese Europe, and Will Marion Cook. We now present to our readers a sketch of the famous Will Tyers, composer, choral conductor and master arranger of music.

According to our biographical source, William H. Tyers was born in Petersburg, Va., in 1870, but his parents moved to New York City. While a boy Tyers showed a remarkable genius for composition, and at the age of 17 had composed quite a number of polkas, waltzes and so forth. In 1390 he toured Europe, as librarian in a musical company, and while in Germany he studied instrumentation under Gaspari. Ill health compelled him to return to America, and since then he has devoted his entire time to composing, writing and arranging music. He has held positions as musical arranger in a number of the leading music publishing houses of New York, and is said to be the best-trained musical arranger of his race. He has been in popular demand for years by some of the leading stars in many of the musical productions, to arrange their music. "Trocha" (a Cuban dance) was the first composition that made real fame for Tyers; it was played by the leading bands and orchestras of the country; since then he has written quite a number of other characteristic dances like the the Dance Phillipine, La Mariposa, La Coqueta, Maori and Panama. Mr. Tyers was assistant conductor of the Clef Club, and the New York *Evening Post* said of his latest composition as played at the recent Carnegie Hall concert: (*ee sketch of James Rees Europe.*) "Were the name of Strauss appended to the Tout a Vous waltz by Tyers it would be one of the most popular waltzes in the world to-day."

Will Tyers is an important one of the group already presented, and who have banded themselves together for a better uplift and brighter musical future for the race. There are many other lights, like Will Vodery; Chris' Smith etc., who, owing to time, will not be presently considered. But we hope to publish for the benefit of our readers, as early as possible, sketches as exemplary Lessons from the Life and Works of S. Coleridge-Taylor.

Buckle Down.

(From The Pathfinder.)

Buckle down and meet it whatever it may be,
Nothing's very easy, though we make it so with glee,
Buckle down and face it with the sunshine on your shield.
If you buckle down and meet it, there,s a chance that it will yield.
Buckle down! What magic in that challenge to our strength!
The call that comes to every man of energy at length.
Buckle down in earnest if you want to win the goal;
Buckle down to duty if you care for heart and soul.
Buckle down and beat it with the force of all your will;
Buckle down and conquer every shadow of the ill;
No-one makes a highway to the dreams that shall come true
Till he buckles down in earnest to be the things there are todo,
—Baltimore Sun.

War Costs Heavy in Switzerland.

(From The Pathfinder.)

Switzerland. The war has caused serious financial losses to Swiss railroad companies and proprietors of hotels. Owing to the dwindling of the tourist business the hotel keepers estimate that their business has already fallen off $100,000,000 while the secondary railways, including the funiculars, have lost about a fourth of that amount as a result of the reduction in both passenger and freight traffic.

Up to the end of October the cost of guarding the country's neutrality had amounted to $51,000,000 and it is estimated by the Swiss treasury department that at the end of the second year of the war, if it con-

Figure 4.1 Page 2 of *The Herald*, 8 March 1916.
Reprinted courtesy of The Danish Royal Library, Mediastream.

by slaveholders to manage their captives less than one hundred forty years earlier. The Labour Union strike campaign, it would seem, was a means of regulating the plantation owners' conduct. Although it may have appeared 'hot' or harsh, Jackson argued, this was nothing compared to what the people were due. This is an altogether different tenor from the appeasing – if at times ironic – tone regarding interrelational respect that is present in Jackson's editorials concerning racial relationships on the islands. The new tone speaks on several levels of hypomnesis: first, in the documentation found in the writing both of the regulations of conduct and of the newspaper; second, in the inscription on the body, the mark left by the slave owners' cruelty, which was carried on into memory and surviving bodies; and third, the lingering trace, idea or notion that 'the planter will bear . . . to their grave'. The editorial may be understood as an archivization, a technology of subjectivity grounded in the historical past as well as within living memory. Like the editorial's referencing of documents, inscriptions and traces, the reader would be reminded of the shared past and be able to understand her embodied subjectivity as a material heritage of slavery.

Unpacking this, Jackson first published the historical documentation of slaveholders' cruelty against enslaved labourers alongside another – arguably equally historical – document: the editorial defending the labourers' strike. The juxtaposition of the two documents highlighted how one claimed domination through physical power while the other claimed rights through a tough campaign when reason failed. One pointed to the past and the other to the future, simultaneously claiming that '[t]he conduct of the planters today is very near the same as it used to be in 1783', thereby creating commonality and warning against complacency. Jackson could have simply referred to the well-known regulations, but by juxtaposing the two documents, he advanced an intertextual discourse, the materialisation of which is found in the bodily marks from slavery that were still present in Jackson's St. Croix, particularly among labourers. The marks that Jackson described are painfully palpable in the text of the 1783 regulations, but they are also brought into the present of *The Herald* and the labour strike. The marks were present in the form of scars from whips and pinches but were also present in the very bodies of the islands' population, the editorial stated. 'The origin of mulattos' and their bodies are the marks and markers of rape and sexual torture inscribed upon the bodies to come by the cruelty of the past, Jackson insisted. By painstakingly reproducing the regulations, Jackson insisted upon the materiality of the memory and perhaps its power to produce political change. Finally, Jackson hinted at a trace stemming from the labour strike and the conduct of both the labourers and the plantation owners: A lingering idea, a change or transformation, will follow from the strike and be borne by the Crucian population to come: the mark of a labourers' rising, of rights being claimed, struggles being fought and progress being made.

Jackson argued that the Labour Union's accomplishment would transform the relationship between labourers and planters on the islands. The strike will have proven the labourers as equally important to production and underscore both sides' interdependence. Importantly, the traces of slavery regulations and punishments that existed in the Crucian present included ideas and notions – and did not result in retaliation or violence against the slave and plantation owners. Whereas enslavement was built upon violence and corporeal dehumanisation, the struggle for civil rights was built upon reason and, if that failed, metaphors and memories. The combined reference to the past and to its persistence in the present grounded Jackson's editorial and replaced the otherwise-favoured language and ideals of equality and freedom. Appealing to justice and respect had been 'proved fruitless', and Jackson's editorial broke free from abstractions. The editorial may, then, also be read as a vernacular expression of the changing same. Mirroring the editorial text with the historical text of regulations, Jackson creates a document that draws upon the collective memory and lived experience of its African Caribbean readers, yet the reproduction of the historical text also acquires a new meaning in the political context of the strike. It is a meaning that grants strength and hope despite the pain attached to the memory. The editorial and the accompanying text thereby allow Jackson to archive the 'Laws Used for Regulating the Conduct of Slaves' within an African Caribbean experience, reclaiming it and assigning it a political role in the service of those who previously suffered under it.

The pain the laws had inflicted was still carried as marks on the readers' bodies. Their physical connection to the memory of slavery was evoked and re-membered by the text, reminding readers that political acts make a social difference through embodied efforts. The editorial envisions a potential future: not merely a resolution to the strike but a possibility of seeing the community anew, as a formation of identification and subjectivity.

THE DECLARATION OF INDEPENDENCE

Following the strike, talk of selling the islands resurfaced. The question of whether Denmark should sell the islands to the Americans had previously been discussed on two occasions, most recently in 1902 when the decision did not successfully pass through Danish parliament,[6] and the sale was rejected. Now it seemed the perfect time for the Danes: The United States wanted the islands in their possession because of their strategic – in terms of access and territory relating to the war which the United States was about to enter – location, and the Danes had been losing money on the islands since the mid-nineteenth century when slavery had been abolished and sugar production shifted from cane-based production to the use of beets. Abolition, of course, also ended the free exploitation of human labour in the sugar plantations and rum production. Moreover, the islands' governor Helweg-Larsen and his colleagues were disseminating the ideas that Jackson and his peers were 'revolting', leaving the island in a state of emergency. They called upon the Danish government to send a warship, *Valkyrien*, to the island to protect the plantation owners and landowners, and *The Herald* reported that they even briefly brought martial law to the island (25.2.16).

The sale of the islands was decided in August 1916.[7] Almost a year passed before *The Herald* is again to be found on microfilm in the Danish archives. During the years of Danish rule, Jackson was requested to send three copies of every issue of *The Herald* to the Danish administration, a practice that he alleged in *The Herald* caused him to work overtime and definitely conjured up conspiracy theories of surveillance of the paper (30.6.16).[8] The United States seemed not to have such rigorous filing practices, and the issues available on microfilm thin out from 1917 to 1925. On 10 June 1925, the daily issue is inexplicably the last available copy.

On 3 July 1917, Emancipation Day,[9] and just short of a year after the first official messages about the pending sale began coming in, *The Herald* filled its front page and second page with another reprint. This time the reprinted text was The Declaration of Independence, followed by an editorial explaining its historical context. The Declaration was from 1776 and therefore hardly news, yet the reprint served to teach readers about the new Mother Country and its values of freedom and pursuit of happiness, which Jackson shared. Indeed, America's Declaration of Independence from the United Kingdom seemed historically fitting, bearing in mind the Crucian hopes for emancipation from under Danish colonial rule. Although the two-and-a-half-page article focussed mainly on the days and politics leading up to the signing of the historical document, Jackson changed his tenor a little over halfway through the contextual, historical essay. He wrote:

> No one, after reading the Declaration of Independence, can fail to admit that America was justified in the course pursued. No one can fail to admire the manly courage with which they braved the wrath of their powerful mother.
> Today we see the glorious Star-Spangled Banner waving over us. We know that all the ties that bound us to a European government have been broken. The name 'Danish West Indies' has been changed to 'Virgin Islands of the United States'. But the atmosphere remains the same. The Americans are here; the spirit of Americanism is absent. We live here under the sovereignty of a republican form of government but the subservient monarchiel customs and its laws are still scourging us with its prickly tail. (3.7.17)

Despite the name change and the knowledge as well as familiarity of the great American democracy, this remained out of reach for inhabitants of the US Virgin Islands. Jackson wrote:

> Santa Crucians wish they could feel happy. But how can we? The pain is greater than before. The days seem longer and more dreary. Liberty is in sight; we beckon it; we try to reach it. But like some enchanted object we can not lay hold of it.
> Santa Crucians want to rejoice. But how can we, when those oppressive laws of the period of slavery are yet in force. (3.7.17)

The powers that be had washed their hands of the situation, and the inhabitants of St. Croix had been left with the same old laws, regulations and practices as under colonial rule. Indeed, Jackson wrote, some conditions seemed to have deteriorated, such as increasing rates of imprisonment and the public humiliation of female convicts, which even the Danish public deplored. The Crucians were not happy, and Jackson wrote in conclusion that 'for a fact we shall be carrying bleeding hearts below smiling faces'.

This pointed juxtaposition of The Declaration of Independence, in which Americans rejoiced, and the editorial, which recounted the continued struggle of the Crucians, bears similarities to the juxtaposition of the 'Laws Used for Regulating the Conduct of Slaves' with Jackson's editorial the year before. As with the 'Laws Used for Regulating the Conduct of Slaves', The Declaration of Independence lists injustices and violations against an oppressed people: injustices against the Americans by the British,

Figure 4.2 Front page of *The Herald*, 3 July 1917.
Reprinted courtesy of The Danish Royal Library, Mediastream.

and violations against the enslaved people of St. Croix by the Danes. But whereas the former is celebrated by the formerly oppressed because these injustices were overcome, the latter is a recurring reminder inscribed in the bodies of descendants. Although the ideal of overcoming injustice is universalised in the former in the words 'We hold these truths to be self-evident, that all men are created equal, that they are endowed by their Creator with certain unalienable rights, that among these are life, liberty and the pursuit of happiness', the editorial makes clear the limitations of these words. 'The rights of the people to alter or to abolish' a destructive government belongs to a different people. The words of the embodied not-yet-citizen of St. Croix are heartbreaking not just on account of the hopeless yearnings of the Crucians but also because of the realisation of the inadequacy of ideology. It would seem that agitation requires local democracy and real bodies and minds – situatedness and embodiedness – if ideals are to be realised. Despite all his intentions and hopes for the future of his people and the island, the transfer had proven less successful than Jackson had hoped in terms of his dreams for the future of his island and his people. The editorial intervention on 3 July is political and a claim to citizenship not because of its recitation of The Declaration of Independence but because of its pain and its continued struggle in the underdog position of the constant counterpublic of the African Caribbean people.

Similar to the editorial concerning the strike, this text presented the past side by side with the present. But in contrast to the 'Laws Used for Regulating the Conduct of Slaves', The Declaration of Independence was a memory and political act of another people and other bodies, and the melancholia engulfing Jackson's writing on the lost enchantment of the American spirit is a cry for a past that never was. Jackson can no longer use a shared history to demonstrate the embodiment of his journalism, thereby producing a vernacular expressive culture. It becomes painfully clear that The Declaration of Independence is built around a modern mantra that favours a universal standard of man specific to the Western, white male. This is precisely the standard that is used to bring about hierarchies between people, calling them into sexualised, racialised and naturalised power structures.

WHAT IS A US CITIZEN?

The editorial featuring The Declaration of Independence is also indicative of Jackson's struggle to find his editorial and political feet in the age of US freedom. The editorials and articles gained a distinctly professional layout, and stories on the plight of people of African descent tended towards narratives of lynchings and killings in the United States rather than achievements and creativity and the relationship with Harlem. Whereas articles in pre-transfer issues of *The Herald* were inspired by tales of success and of cultural prowess in America, in contrast to the exploitation of labourers that occurred on St. Croix, they now focussed on the common political plight of people of African descent in the United States – their hardships and struggle. America was no longer the land of dreams but instead one of reality – or at least a version of reality. The war years stifled editorial and journalistic expressions, and the long, dreary days seemed to be spent reflecting upon the true meaning of these fine ideologies and rights claims. Upon request from a reader, on 14 and 17 February 1919, Jackson engaged in an analysis of what was entailed in the differences between the categories of citizens, nationals and subjects, and he found that the positions of those under US rule were dependent upon their positions under Danish rule. When the islands' administration was transferred to the Americans, their citizens were able to keep their Danish citizenship if they made arrangements for this before the end of the first year following ratification of the agreement between Denmark and the United States. If they made no such arrangements, they would be citizens of the United States. Danish subjects, however, would be citizens of the US Virgin Islands, which fell under the Organic Act rather than the Constitution. They would not be citizens of the United States, and their 'civil rights and political status' (6.8.17; 17.2.19) would be determined by Congress. But were the African

Caribbean population on St. Croix citizens or subjects under Danish rule? Jackson believed they were citizens, although his analysis here was not entirely convincing, and Danish scholars continue to discuss the civil rights of descendants of enslaved people in the colonies and in Denmark (Nielsen 2016).

Jackson's argument for why African Caribbean people were Danish citizens was that Danish law made no distinction between subject and citizen, and some would argue that, according to the letter of the law, the Crucians were citizens. It is also likely that the English text and the colonial practices obscured the lack of privileges and rights afforded to the population of African descent – that is, the practice of civil rights was curtailed by cultural habits and racist assumptions. Indeed, despite the fact that most of the African Caribbean inhabitants were born on the islands, they did not enjoy suffrage under Danish rule, which is why Jackson specifically urged the king of Denmark to change this practice when he visited Denmark in 1915. The king did not comply, and the fight for citizenship continued for Jackson. However, unlike his pre-transfer political fights for the labourers, which drew upon a memory of enslavement and oppression, this fight was based on scholarly analyses of legal texts and testimonies before the congressional committee sent to the island in early February 1920. On 9 February, the US congressional committee was welcomed to the islands. The committee was there to discuss the rights and obligations of the islanders under US jurisdiction, and Jackson was in high spirits with hopes for reform. His hopes, however, were dashed once again when the committee ended up recommending every reform Jackson had wished for – except citizenship and the rights this entailed (6.5.20). The words of The Declaration of Independence did not match the reality of Jackson's longed-for Americanism. Suffrage was vital to the American spirit (23.9.20), and Jackson took up this topic again and again, at least until the publication of the last available issues of *The Herald* in the archives. Yet at the same time as he praised American suffrage, Jackson began calling the United States the 'occupier' of the territory, rather than the Mother Country (cf. 11.4.22; 27.10.23). On 20 April 1922, Jackson was sentenced to prison for an article that set forth the proceedings of a police court. The editorial in which this news was relayed continued by urging the reader to reflect upon the role of the press.

Even before this sad news, times had been hard for *The Herald*. Subscribers did not pay their bills, and production prices were rising. *The Herald* did not, however, demand more money of its subscribers because:

> *The Herald* is the people's paper. It is not a class paper. In order that it may reach the people the subscription rate has been kept far below that of other papers. . . . When the poor man can't read *The Herald* there's no meaning in printing it. (7.7.17)

The war also had an impact on the content of *The Herald*: Jackson and his colleagues were unable to publish the usual notifications of ship arrivals and departures as well as of embarkations and disembarkations. Moreover, Jackson had been threatened and believed that 'it is dangerous to run a newspaper, as a newspaper ought to be run these days' (21.3.19). What is left of the political when the political act of printing is stifled, when the body is jailed or transposed to another political and geographical context, such as the lynchings in the United States, and when the political aims have become abstract paintings of ideal declarations from someone else's past? Arguably, by this time, Jackson was no longer practicing citizen journalism because he was no longer embodied in the struggle. He had achieved Americanism only to discover that it muffled his distinct political voice.

In its final three years of publication, scholarly suffrage campaigns became a staple of *The Herald*, and Jackson continued to argue that it was necessary for the press to give voice to the disenfranchised (6.5.22). He called out the double standards, of which he had arguably also been a victim, of teaching schoolchildren about the Constitution while refusing to bring the islands under that same law (cf. 13.5.22; 28.7.22). Indeed, he thundered, 'We are not satisfied with' the Naval administration (17.5.22). Jackson's disenchantment with the American administration inspired a new form of localism in which he sought to bring the words of The Declaration of Independence to bear on the Crucian administration. Whereas Jackson's earlier Labour Union work had focussed on labourers' conditions and connected their plight directly to that of their enslaved forbearers (8.3.16), the people's press now oriented itself towards the more diffuse group of 'taxpayers' and 'Santa Cruzians', inspired perhaps by the language of The Declaration of Independence:

> It is the universal principle that the tax payer has the right through the newspaper to ask questions on public matters involving the expenditure of public monies, and we are going to exercise our rights and that of the taxpayers of the community in which we intend to live and die as Santa Cruzians, if not as Americans. (25.5.22)

This embrace of American universalism and civic duties and benefits divorces the particularity of the African-Caribbean body and experience from the article's rights claim and striving for justice. The end of the quote, however, circles back and insists on the universal standards of governing for St. Croix in particular, if not as part of US jurisdiction. In this manner, Jackson adopted universal principles based on the white, American, male body for the local administration and governance of the islands. The disenchantment that is so evident in the editorial concerning The Declaration of Independence is maintained over the following years. It becomes clear that Jackson's rights claims can no longer be connected to the embodied memory and lived experience of the African Caribbean people, which has become an artificial appendix to the African American struggle at best and at worse a question of semantics in legal texts. The pronouncement of the readers as taxpayers and citizens of their local public also points to a new role Jackson carved out in the United States years.

MEMORIES OF A SHARED HISTORY

Despite their differences in content, the two documents – the 'Laws Used for Regulating the Conduct of Slaves' and The Declaration of Independence – both document and thereby materialise history. Whereas the colonial regulations on punishments also represent cultural memory borne by St. Croix's African Caribbean labourers, The Declaration of Independence can be said to be the memory of another people: eighteenth-century Englishmen's memories and ideals, the memories of people of privilege, despite their oppression by the British Crown. This difference is, however, not simply a difference of ethnicity, historical era and power. It is a difference between the particular experience and the universal ideology. It is not that Jackson did not share the ideology and sentiment of freedom held by the English; indeed, he underscored the righteousness with which the US forefathers authored and signed The Declaration of Independence. Rather, what stops Jackson from associating The Declaration of Independence with the political aims of the Crucian people is that it belonged to another body and could leave no discernible trace in the hearts and minds of the inhabitants of St. Croix and its sister islands. Despite Jackson's attempts at adopting universal principles and adapting them to Crucian tradition, The Declaration of Independence never seems to be of and for the people of St. Croix.

The Declaration of Independence also belonged to a nation – the United States of America – and Jackson knew from his struggles to become a citizen of that nation what obstacles he faced. More than that, however, in comparison to the national cry for independence from the United Kingdom, the editorial built upon the 'Laws Used for Regulating the Conduct of Slaves' drew political and social connections with two cosmopolitan or transnational movements: socialism and the civil rights movement. From the struggles expressed in the 1916 labour strike editorial to the 1917 editorial regret for the lack of Americanism, Jackson's arguments for liberties and opportunities as law-abiding citizens shifted from a cosmopolitan perspective to a national scope. Paradoxically, by becoming part of the desired American political spectrum, Jackson became cut off from expressing the grounded cosmopolitanism that formed the political act of *The Herald*'s first year and a half while under Danish colonial rule.[10] By evoking the atrocities of slavery in the 1916 editorial on the strike, Jackson used the collective memory in the hypomnesic event to propel new thoughts and imaginations as to who the Crucians were and could become. The whispers of the archives were clear because they were connected to remembering bodies and minds – painfully so. This was an embodied creativity and expression that The Declaration of Independence did not permit Jackson and his peers. The processes of archivization differ despite their common structure of argument and plant-based artefactual materialisation: paper. The difference is the body of lived experience.

The two events, written hypomneses, transformed Crucian society, and in particular the African Caribbean population, into achieved, cultural citizens in the first instance, making its claim to the right to be treated fairly, and sunk it into melancholia in the second instance when the ideals of national liberty proved unachievable. Both editorials testify to the struggles of achieving rights and liberties as citizens, but they do so in different ways due to the political, embodied and situated nature of the events and due to the archivization and remembering processes upon which the editorials drew. Yet the archivization process, which the availability of the digital microfilm produced, opens our eyes to the historicity of citizen journalism. As a product of journalism, *The Herald* was both a first draft of history and a material commemoration of the past, continuously transposing its always-relevant relation to the future. By mirroring political acts on historical documents, Jackson could be said to create a gesture: a format that – when repeated – amplified and restructured the message to encompass an imaginative expression of a potential future. The gesture is a performance as well as an act. Importantly, a gesture is embodied. A similar concept of gesture is discernible in contemporary citizen journalism. In chapter 5, I explore the implications of this archivization process going forward when I bring the postcolonial conceptualisation developed in this chapter into the contemporary practice of digital political acts.

NOTES

1. In their inspiring argument, Shakuntala Rao and Herman Wasserman (2007) discuss the problem of universalising concepts of 'truth' in journalism and analyse instead the possible uses of concepts such as dharma and Ubuntu. These concepts are seen as similar to the Western idea of cosmopolitanism, in which a universal ethics is sought. However, Rao and Wasserman observe that, whereas cosmopolitanism is founded on individualism and the individual's rights and freedoms, dharma and Ubuntu take a community-oriented perspective. Few theorists, however, take into account the journalism produced by citizens of colonial spaces.

2. The documents are available at the National Archives, Washington: http://www.archives.gov/ and Rigsarkivet, Copenhagen: http://www.virgin-islands-history.org/en/about/the-historical-material-about-denmarks-time-in-the-west-indies/.

3. Although Jackson cut a divisive political figure, he was also known as 'the Moses of his people' in St. Croix.

4. Due to the 2017 centenary celebrating the transfer from Danish to US jurisdiction, publications on Jackson and his Labour Union work have been produced. See for instance Erik Gøbel (2017).

5. Importantly, hybridity and creolisation to thinkers such as Glissant are exactly rhizomatic in structure (see Glissant 2007).

6. Back then, Denmark had a two-house system akin to that of the United Kingdom, and while the decision was passed by *Folketinget*, it was rejected by *Landstinget*.

7. See chapter 3 for more details on Jackson's position on the sale.

8. However, it is worth noting that every newspaper and journal in Denmark is required to register and be archived – even the most local and politically insignificant publications are archived in the National Archives, today also. The fact that the administration wanted the names of all the subscribers of *The Herald* may reasonably give pause, as it did (30.6.16).

9. It is difficult to say why Jackson chose to publish an editorial on the Declaration of Independence the day prior to the independence celebrations. In the available copies of *The Herald* there is no indication that Emancipation Day – the 3rd of July – was celebrated in public, and the editorial does not make any mention of emancipation from enslavement 3 July 1848. However, the coincidence gives pause to the meaning of independence to Jackson, although he does not seem to underscore the significance.

10. See chapter 3.

5

Citizen Journalism and the Politics of Visibility

> When there is a common space of appearance, common sensation, and common consent, its potential can be framed by the photograph. . . . That common sensation occurs when we see, in the sense of coming to understand, a photograph *of* the space of appearance that emanates *from* the space of appearance, contains its potential and is not simply *about* it (as in the form of photojournalism).
>
> —Nicholas Mirzoeff, *The Appearance of Black Lives Matter*, 40

In his work on visuality, Nicholas Mirzoeff does not use the idea of a space of appearance in the manner originally developed by Hannah Arendt (1958) or as Roger Silverstone (2007) and Lilie Chouliaraki (2013a) have brought it to bear on media ethics and politics of pity. Mirzoeff thinks of a space of appearance as a reoccurring event in which embodied and situated expressions lay the groundwork for political manifestations and desires for social change. The space of appearance is thus akin to the Deleuzian concept of recurrent events, which are processes of becoming and repeatable in different settings, times and spaces (Patton 2006).[1] Because of the singular nature of an event, a space of appearance cannot occur in surveillance mode or as a disciplinary tool, running on contingencies and causalities over time. Furthermore, it is not about coming to a consensus on a topic or interrogating and discussing social and political issues, as in the classical understanding of a public sphere or even an agonistic or participatory space in which debates and standpoints are held up to scrutiny. Mirzoeff's space of appearance emanates from that about which it speaks. It is a situated knowledge: grounded in the local community, embodied in the people affected and encouraging concrete political actions and change. The space of appearance is about being able to appear not as an object, represented by others or participating on their terms, but as a political, collective and social subject. The space of appearance relates to a politics of visibility, or visuality, in Mirzoeff's terms, yet following the logic of the space of appearance, visuality is more than just rights to representation and participation. It is instead an aesthetic order among people comprised of structures of visibility and invisibility that classify and separate individuals into grievable, political lives and culturally objectified lives, thereby generating a 'complex of visuality' (Mirzoeff 2011, 34). Leaning on a definition of Foucault's Benthamian panopticon as a disciplinary mechanism based on the 'eyes that must see without being seen' (Foucault 1977, 171), visuality, like surveillance, is a disciplinary power that normalises judgement and functions as a 'value-giving' measure. As a result, 'the perpetual penalty [of] the disciplinary institutions compares, differentiates, hierarchizes, homogenizes, excludes. In short, it *normalizes*' (Foucault 1977, 183; italics in original). This is what Mirzoeff identifies as the space of *non*-appearance: It goes beyond the visual and enters the mind to become ideology. Indeed, Mirzoeff (2017a, 118) calls the space of non-appearance 'America', underscoring that he is referring not to a geographical place but to a state of understanding. Jackson's yearning for 'Americanism' in his editorial on the first Fourth of July celebration on the Caribbean islands in 1917[2] and Mirzoeff's critique of 'America' as an ideology of capitalism and commercialism favoured over the voices and politics of the African American civil rights movement Black Lives Matter in 2017 obviously differ dramatically in terms of their perspectives on a space of appearance and a space of non-appearance. Arguably, Mirzoeff's and Jackson's changing perspectives on what they regard as America/nism represents a movement of conceptual deterritorialization, uprooting the ideal of America/nism in order to see the structures of surveillance and discipline that underlie it. In her seminal work on the political ramifications of conflict images and frames of war, Judith Butler (2009, 12) suggests that 'it is not only a question of finding new content, but also of working with received renditions of reality to show how [the frames] can and do break with themselves'. America/nism is in this terminology a framed reality, a complex of visuality for which Jackson yearns and that Mirzoeff rejects. Neither Jackson nor Mirzoeff manage to generate an affirmative movement out of this frame, though Butler suggests that frames may bend and break, creating an opportunity for a space of appearance to emerge. Butler's radical suggestion brings to the fore the agency of frames and with them our received notions of reality – that is, the relationship between spaces of (non-)appearance. This complex of visuality is brought about through circulation and dissemination. Moreover, digital images in particular – because of their material structures as assemblages within this complex – have agency and grant us an unprecedented possibility 'to apprehend something about what or who is living but has not been generally "recognized" as life' (12). For Butler, then, creating a space of appearance where there is none is a political act that establishes the recognisability of the citizen subject. This notion of breaking frames of war could lead to 'alternative readings . . . which might establish new ruptures in our viewing of other people's lives, fundamental to the production and discussion of . . . photographs' (Zarzycka 2012, 73). Visuality – if not surveillance – may, then, be countered by the right to look (Mirzoeff 2011). Mirzoeff argues that in order for visuals and visibility to serve democratic ends, it is necessary for accessibility to extend to more than just image production and circulation. Marginalised individuals and groups must instead be able to claim the right to be seen on their own terms, using their own aesthetics – that is, they must be able to be seen as creating a space of appearance.

Visuality goes beyond vision and encompasses all senses. In Mirzoeff's (2017a, 85) words, it is 'a collective way to look, visualize, and imagine'. Like Braidotti, Mirzoeff (93) stresses the affirmative and creative forces of counter-political spaces. 'Solidarity as a mutual seeing – enabled by social media, which creates a transnational space of appearance that might in turn form a different kind of politics' is a becoming-minoritarian, a continuous reworking of collective – and potentially cosmopolitan – subjectivity (Braidotti 2006a). Memory plays an important role in becoming-minoritarian. It is through the process of archivization that structures of inclusion and exclusion occur and with them the potential to create counter-memories, to break frames and produce spaces of appearance. If the political act raises a rights claim, it is not a legal claim alone but also a cultural and social claim – a claim for subjectivity and recognisability within a self-crafted space of appearance. This space is produced through counter-memories continuously forming subjectivity. A space of appearance 'does not discipline, operate surveillance, or categorize' but instead 'sends messages to the future', Mirzoeff (40) asserts, echoing Braidotti (2006b, 167), who 'stresses the deep generative powers of memory as a political project'.

Although self-defined and self-crafted, the space always already exists in relation to the dominant visuality or majoritarian culture. In the previous analyses, the methodology of this rights claim has been based on the circulation of intertextual discourses, creating counterpublics and drawing upon archival knowledge and understandings as well as contemporary ideological commonalities across national borders. In this chapter, I wish to show how these processes – these conceptual practices that stretch between geographical and temporal spaces – have implications for a present-day understanding of citizen journalism. I have first acknowledged the importance of the concept of visuality and the politics of visibility to present political acts or spaces of appearance today. Second, I argue that similar processes of content and formats creating political acts are at work in Jackson's political writings in *The Herald* and in present-day struggles for civil rights. Finally, I discuss how we may understand images as political acts and as citizen journalism.

I will begin by once again taking up 'Deterritorializing America/nism', extending the findings of chapter 4 that, by 1917, Jackson was no longer practicing citizen journalism but was struggling to find a suitably journalistic tenor to fit his dreams of public voice. Mirzoeff's use of America as a space of non-appearance, an ideology of commercialism that reduces the citizen to a consumer, rests upon the surveillance and disciplining character of public images. In describing the protests that led to the organisation of the Black Lives Matter movement in 2013 and the role played by visibility and invisibility in the life of this new civil rights movement, I will show that Mirzoeff's work is in dialogue with that of Jackson. This does not, of course, mean that Mirzoeff and Jackson agree, as I have already pointed out. Rather, their dialogue can be seen as a deterritorialization of the concept or idea/l of America. While this argument may be said to concern the political spaces or spheres of political acts and appearances, the following section, 'Icons, Gestures and Memory', turns towards the format. As Jackson's *The Herald* drew upon repetitions of historical texts, so have the visual representations that have emerged in the wake of the Black Lives Matter movement drawn upon repeated gestures, performing political acts in social media images. In this chapter, I introduce Black Lives Matter as citizen journalistic practice because the organisation asks the fundamental question also asked by Jackson (and a question I believe to be fundamental to political acts): 'What counts as human?' In order to become a citizen subject, one must first be deemed worthy of a human life. This is not an ideological question that can be readily answered by 'We are all human' or 'All lives matter'. It is an empirical question, one that asks: 'How do we construct human value in our society today?' 'Who is seen to fall below the set bar?' 'What kinds of texts and images are circulated to uphold our perception of the human and human value?' 'What and whose memories are re-created and archived?' These fundamental questions hark back to colonialism and regimes of enslavement when the hierarchies of human lives were laying the groundwork for the later atrocities of the Shoah. In the analysis of images represented in the struggle of the Black Lives Matter movement in this chapter, I argue for the importance of creating forms of expressions that challenge the given frame, either through building upon counter-memory or by insisting upon a vernacular expression as a changing same. That is, I employ the analytical framework proposed in this book to challenge the status quo of public engagement. Finally, in 'Vernacular Expressions: Citizen Media Expressions', I reintroduce Gilroy's concept to broaden the scope of citizen journalism to encompass media and cultural products more generally.

DETERRITORIALIZING AMERICA/NISM

For Jackson, Americanism was democracy, the sense of freedom and equal rights about which he read in The Declaration of Independence. Jackson was striving for an ideal, but he was unable to achieve it, despite St. Croix coming under US jurisdiction in 1917. Jackson clearly saw his role as editor of a leading publication on the islands as aligned with the great hope for democracy. In late August 1917, Jackson took a point of departure in a quote from Thomas Jefferson, stating his supposed preference for newspapers without government to government without newspapers. 'Jefferson recognized the important part the press would play in the republic he was trying to found', Jackson wrote, exalting in the pivotal role of the press as educator and opinion maker. He continued: 'We must prepare ourselves for the responsibilities of the future. We have got to be ready to appreciate the full rights that comes with citizenship of the great republic'. In this logic, it followed that '*The Herald* is therefore to be followed in these days. Be like the American people – read daily papers and digest what you read. . . . *The Herald* gives out the public opinion of this island and will do its utmost to serve all classes' (20.8.17). The editorial is interesting because Jackson explicitly articulates *The Herald*'s shifting focus from first serving an oppositional or counterpublic against organisational powers on the islands to later aspiring to become part of the core of political organisation, the public sphere. For Jackson, becoming American meant becoming a deliberative democracy in which he would be recognised, if not as a citizen, then as a newspaper editor and a respected opinion leader. Jackson understood that becoming a citizen could take time: '[I]t is war time, and all the heads of Government are busy with war questions' (20.8.17). There was, however, no doubt in Jackson's mind that the islands were to be 'Americanized' and that this was a good thing.

The sense of melancholy saturating the editorial of 3 July 1917, when Jackson was celebrating his first Emancipation/Independence Day[3] as an American subject, however, morphed into disappointment and incredulity as time went on. In 1919, Jackson sought to extrapolate meaning from the tangled language of Danish law of the treaty governing the transfer following the islands' sale. The inconsistent and interchangeable use of the terms 'citizens', 'subjects' and 'inhabitants' was confusing, and Jackson struggled with the fact that even if 'Danish natives' (people born on the islands) had been considered Danish citizens prior to the transfer and therefore equal to 'Native Danes' (people who had moved to the islands from Denmark), their 'status was not determined by the Treaty' but by the US Constitution, which stated that only people born in the United States and naturalised inhabitants were citizens of the United States. This, of course, did not apply to the people of St. Croix, who were born either in the Danish colonies or in Denmark or other European countries. Thus, Jackson concluded, 'We are citizens and yet not citizens. Wait' (17.2.19). The frustration is palpable, and the racial fault lines that were washed out by the legal jargon were not lost on him. Such fault lines were moreover echoed in other, later writings on colonial and racial discrimination between those with and those without citizen status (Chakrabarty 2000, Goldberg 2002). Later, Jackson pondered why the children of St. Croix were taught to look up to the ideals of equality and freedom, so eloquently expressed in the Constitution, when they themselves were not allowed to enjoy these same rights and freedoms (cf. 13.5.22; 28.7.22). Americanism came to represent an unreachable ideal, but even more so, it was a lost opportunity for Jackson to play the role he felt called upon to play. Jackson had perhaps hoped that American deliberative democracy would be the great equaliser and would welcome *The Herald* into Thomas Jefferson's utopia in which the press educated and informed the public as well as held politicians accountable. In chapter 4, I wrote that by the time the islands were transferred to US jurisdiction, Jackson was arguably no longer producing citizen journalism. We might add now that his desire for the counter-position of citizen journalism had arguably passed. Yearning for Americanism meant that Jackson relinquished embodied politics in favour of abstract ideals. His quest remained a deliberative and civil government for St. Croix as well as political reforms for the benefit of the Crucians, but his readers went from being labourers and squatters to being 'all classes' (20.8.17). In other words, Jackson wanted to play a role within the space of non-appearance, the space of the public sphere, yet this proved impossible.

When Mirzoeff (2017a, 118), in his detailed analysis of the Black Lives Matter movement in today's United States, calls the space of non-appearance 'America', he argues that the space of appearance – the opportunities to speak and be heard – is colonised by disciplining and surveillance media and politics. The public sphere as a strategy of recognition and voice is to some degree stifling in and of itself because, as Nancy Fraser argues (1990), it is based on the faulty idea of a common good defined by the people or classes in power. I argue that, despite the multiple outlets from which to speak publicly and in different tenors and rhythms today, despite the cacophony of voices, as long as we speak to the deliberative democratic public sphere, the inescapable sense of plenitude will mask silences and absences that are crucial to understanding citizen journalistic practice as political citizenship and subjectivity formation.

As discussed in chapter 2, the public sphere regulates who gets heard and recognised through journalistic news values and practices of participation. The public sphere presents an arena in which differences are bracketed off, and the voices heard are reduced to those that fit the journalistic mould. In effect, journalistic values and the public sphere regulate who appears and whose issues are brought to the table. This also means that in the case of the American press at the time of *The Herald* and arguably today, the professionalisation of the press and its function within the public sphere and the concept of objectivity had already mainstreamed a white majoritarian representation of citizen subjects (Gonzáles and Torres 2011), underscoring the hierarchised categorisations of human subjects in terms of race, gender and sexuality. The hierarchy is re-enacted indirectly through the closed system of what defines the 'common good' and who is granted access to the public sphere. This echoes the question posed in *The Herald* on 16 November 1915, leading up to the strike, and referenced in chapter 4: 'Are the people worthwhile helping?' (16.11.15). Who is sufficiently human to receive attention and appear in public? It is the space of non-appearance – or in Butler's words, 'the norm' – that continuously differentiates between and excludes humans in order to retain control of the definition of normality and the common good. The idea of the human, then, is based on the idea of the non-human. In a deconstructive move, 'the human' is only ever not the non-human. But these definitions are ever changing: 'Some humans take their humanness for granted, while others struggle to gain access to it. The term "human" is constantly doubled, exposing the ideality and coercive character of the norm: some humans qualify as humans; some do not' (Butler 2009, 76). The public sphere accounts for much of these movements of humanness. This is not a critique of journalism as practiced by professionals today. It is instead an extension of the critique of the tenets and logic of modernity supporting the exclusionary public sphere, which in turn is continuously reaffirmed, intentionally or otherwise, through journalistic practices. This is the realm that Mirzoeff calls America without referring to a specific geography. It is the 'maintenance of white supremacy [that] relies on the continued existence and exploitation of spaces of non-appearance' (Mirzoeff 2017a, 137). In naming the public sphere as dependent on white supremacy, Mirzoeff follows up on Gonzáles and Torres's (2011) argument that US media mainstreamed white voices and representation long ago to the detriment of minority voices and spaces.

The space of non-appearance that appears to Mirzoeff in his studies of Black Lives Matter is the set of court transcript documents from the *State of Missouri vs. Darren Wilson* case, following the killing of Michael Brown by then–police officer Wilson in Ferguson in 2014. Mirzoeff's (2017a, 137) analysis of the transcripts reveals how the 'informal structures of inherent racial hierarchy operate' and are obscured. Mirzoeff (138) identifies what he calls the 'New Jim Crow'. The narrative of how Michael Brown died is buried in page after page of testimony and cross-examination, which boil down to a few seconds of action: 'What comes irresistibly to mind is not a motion picture but a cell-phone video of the kind we have seen all too often since Ferguson. It is all too easy to imagine', Mirzoeff writes (171). But the video does not exist because no one filmed the death of Michael Brown, which leaves Mirzoeff to conclude that '[i]nstead, we have these tens of thousands of words, designed to prevent us from seeing that simple sequence, but revealing so much more in the process. Keep looking' (2017a, 171). In his analysis, then, Mirzoeff calls on us to remember a sequence of digitalised moving imagery that never existed in order to allow the emergence of what happened to Michael Brown. For Mirzoeff, there is an almost visceral connection between experience, memory and image technology. That is, Mirzoeff's analysis invokes a conceptualisation of memory that contains both unconscious and conscious traces of experiences that may or may not pertain to one's individual life experiences. It does, however, pertain to our collective memory today, for example, following instances of filmed police brutality, particularly against young African American men, which have surfaced since 2014. As discussed in chapter 4, the conceptualisation of memory here relies on the ability of humans to creatively remember things that did not actually happen to them individually (Braidotti 2006b, 166–69) in order to '[a]ccount . . . backwards for the affective impact of various items or data upon oneself [that] is the process of remembering' (173). This is the becoming-minoritarian that forces us to question differentiations and exclusions within the hierarchy of humanness. Mirzoeff uses 'vision' 'in the sense of coming to understand' (2017a, 40) to account backwards and into the future, seeking the technology-infused experience that 'we have seen all too often since Ferguson' (171), to make visible that which is hidden in the documents: the visual experience of Michael Brown's death, the space in which Michael Brown appears.

America/ness, the space that seeks to appear transparent while operating silently to hierarchise and structuralise relations between and among people, may also be understood as a frame that allows for a certain perspective – and not others. These frames and hierarchies persist despite the abundance of images experienced today every time we engage within the structural space of the public sphere. They are politics of visibility that function on the levels of multiplicity and materiality of digital access and availability (Blaagaard, Mortensen and Neumayer 2017). The deterritorialization of America/nism consists of probing questions directed at the concept and its ideals, shifting its meaning and detaching it from the abstract consensus of the public sphere. Though neither Jackson nor Mirzoeff produce an affirmative creativity or re-membering out of the rubble of America/nism, the politics of visibility may be challenged by forging a space of appearance either through vernacular expressions, cultural and visual products and citizen journalism or through a counter-reading and counter-memory. This analysis shifts the perspective and allows thinking to become a form of activism.

ICONS, GESTURES AND MEMORY

If Jackson's readings of the 'Laws for Regulating the Conduct of Slaves' alongside the 1916 Labour Union strike and The Declaration of Independence alongside the experience of being a not-yet-citizen of the desired America in 1917 can be said to draw upon memory to produce textual rights claims, imagery that repeats or mimics previous representations may similarly be understood as rights claims. In relation to the civil rights movement of Black Lives Matter, several images have surfaced and circulated as iconic and politically charged reminders of the struggle and injustice of the racial system in place in the United States. The images are often produced by professional photographers at demonstrations and events. In seeking to understand how these images forge spaces of appearance and may be said to represent citizen journalism, I focus in the section below on two kinds of imagery in relation to memory: the repetition of embodied gesture and the representation of an individual person facing weaponised obstacles. I explore the extent to which these images may be seen as iconic or as appropriations, but I also seek to understand what makes this imagery question the hierarchised categories of the racialised human in different ways. I thus begin by presenting the key work on icons by Robert Hariman and John Louis Lucaites (2007) in which they argue for the civic and social role of (iconic) photojournalism. Their position will help me illustrate how and why two selected kinds of imagery depicting the work of Black Lives Matter (the gesture of raised hands in a repetition of Brown's final attempted gesture and the imagery showing an individual person facing multiple and often weaponized police officers) cannot be iconic in the general sense used by Hariman and Lucaites and may instead represent appropriations of icons, in their terminology. In my reading, Hariman and Lucaites's definition of iconic photojournalism corresponds to a reproduction of the familiar and therefore to the upholding of a visual public sphere.

Hariman and Lucaites's (2007) sustained analysis of iconic images is based on the premise that photojournalism, particularly iconic photojournalism, supports liberal democratic society by serving as the glue that holds democracy together. Images, they argue, reproduce public visuality and invite participants to engage through appropriations and republication of images. That is, an iconic image is iconic partly due to its replicability and appropriations (see also Mortensen 2017). These modalities allow people to partake in shaping society and our common imaginary while drawing upon already established contingencies. Iconic images, Hariman and Lucaites argue, are 'an aesthetically familiar form of civic performance coordinating an array of semiotic transcriptions that project an emotional scenario to manage a basic contradiction or recurrent crisis' (29). Hariman and Lucaites discuss five elements of iconic imagery at length. Here, it will suffice to briefly discuss the first three in particular and in terms of the poststructuralist thinking that has thus far set the tone of critique in this book.

First, iconic images are seen as producing 'aesthetic familiarity', which Hariman and Lucaites (2007, 30) regard as 'representing events according to conventions'. At first glance, then, it would appear that Hariman and Lucaites's conceptualisation of iconic images and photojournalism more broadly is built upon the premise of the public sphere and deliberative democratic participation. If iconic photographs are iconic because they are immediately recognisable rather than disruptive or surprising to the viewer, then their qualities are necessarily those of accustomed visuality and cannot be considered political beyond the public sphere or as producing a space of appearance. Second, Hariman and Lucaites's (33) conceptualisation of 'civic performance' follows the same logic: Performativity is the citation of the same that (re)produces the public, and although 'both error and dissent' are possible, it is mainly to be understood as modalities of political strategy in which errors and dissent may be used to frame reality in accordance with or decidedly against pre-established politics. Similarly, participants or the audience, as Hariman and Lucaites (33–34) refer to them, may intervene but will only be recognised publicly insofar as they adhere to social codes: 'Political identity grows out of the social practices of particular peoples in specific places as they become known to themselves in the communicative media that articulate a culture'. These social codes are semiotically transcribed and articulate 'romance, tragedy, gender, class, nationalism, technocracy, and many other forms of collective organization' (34). It seems impossible to break away from the hegemonic frame or for the frame itself to bend (cf. Butler 2009). Even when appropriations are applied to highlight gender, ethnicity and race, Hariman and Lucaites (43) initially argue for a depoliticised reading:

> To take a specific example, the Iwo Jima icon is celebrated for its egalitarian ethos, yet it also appears to be a picture of white men. The picture could imply that only such men were qualified for citizenship or contributing to the war effort, although that would hardly fit with its use by government to maintain public support for the war. The rhetorical problem is that affirmation of the principle of equality is necessary for both legitimacy and social cohesion in a democratic society, but that principle has no motivational power without social embodiment, which always will be limited to some and exclude others.

This problem persists even in gendered and racial appropriations of the image. Hariman and Lucaites thus regard critical antiracist readings of the image of Iwo Jima as misinterpretations, given that the image has been used to gather public support for war. However, this argument disregards the fact that the abstract notion of the public in the public sphere may be conceived of as white, insofar as whiteness represents universality. If the critique of the public sphere, presented by Gonzáles and Torres as well as by Mirzoeff, is taken into account, then the image of the flag raising on Iwo Jima may be both an image of the whiteness of America and an image designed to gather support for the continued war. Hariman and Lucaites (43) argue that 'some forms of public address may prove better suited than others' and that some forms would be perceived 'to be means of distortion and manipulation rather than rational deliberation': 'The widely disseminated visual image provides the public audience with a sense of shared experience that anchors the necessarily impersonal character of public discourse in the motivational ground of social life'. That is, in the US public sphere, white is considered universal and all-encompassing, so the white soldiers of Iwo Jima represent all colours and citizens.

Hariman and Lucaites then closely follow Habermas in bracketing off difference as inconsequential and therefore the common good as an understanding reached through deliberation among people of universal sameness. While some images' qualities of iconicity (and not others) may seem to come naturally, the selectivity eventually raises questions concerning the terms by which particular images come to be viewed as representational of society and common interests. Why do some images become iconic? (Mortensen 2017). Furthermore, might the common interest and recognisability of certain images over others be grounded not only in majority but also in the power of definition? That is, would the flag over Iwo Jima have been considered iconic in the first place had it portrayed African American servicemen? Would they have appealed to the 'necessarily impersonal character of public discourse' and been able to represent 'social life' in general? Hariman and Lucaites's insistence on a depoliticising of images, their circulation and their production as well as the authors' exclusion of power from their analyses leave the audience and viewers of images powerless, despite their access to technology and potential ability to (re)appropriate icons. The only way audiences can intervene and use iconic images to further their political causes is through appropriations, and 'such variations can only be persuasive if the original model is widely recognized and valued' (288). This means that audiences are doomed to respond to pre-established power relations and are incapable of creating original political acts. Hariman and Lucaites (28–29) defend their stance by critiquing cultural studies' critical readings of technology and representation, arguing that these lead to preconceived conclusions and misconceptions about media communication power. Critical readings may or may not have been unnecessarily dogmatic when it comes to understanding the impact of mass media and communication technologies in the past, yet Hariman and Lucaites arguably throw the baby out with the bathwater when their analyses dismiss the ability of othered identity formations and political subjectivities to be recognised as significant. They regret that no images of civil rights struggles or images from the feminist movement make it to the top tier of iconic imagery, but they seem to miss the point that the necessity of mainstream acceptability for iconicity may have less to do with the number of people subscribing to the 'mainstream' and more to do with the political, social and economic power they possess. In other words, in the United States – which is the focus of their study – the mainstream is white, male and conservative, despite the fact that white, conservative men do not form the majority of the population.

However, Hariman and Lucaites's notion of the iconic image and photojournalism provides a very helpful starting point for analysing the political act of Black Lives Matter imagery. Some imagery produced by Black Lives Matter's political acts may indeed not be recognised as iconic precisely because of the prevalent conceptualisation of iconicity favoured by Hariman and Lucaites. The imagery has nevertheless been termed iconic from time to time and therefore invites exploration into how iconicity may play out beyond the mainstream. It would also seem that the rigid frame of Hariman and Lucaites's definition of the icon does allow for bending or breaking if perspectives are shifted from a political public sphere to a public of counter-subjectivities. In the following, then, I turn my attention to, first, imagery that portrays a lone figure – often a woman – facing a number of weaponised police officers. These images are often labelled as iconic, and I explore whether this may be due to the fact that the images may be read not as political acts but as appropriations of the iconic image from the Tiananmen Square protest of 1989. Second, I look at the gesture made by Black Lives Matter members and allies as a demonstration against injustice and police brutality following the acquittal of officer Darren Wilson in 2014. The gesture amounts to raising both hands, often accompanied by placards with the text 'Hands up! Don't shoot!' Using Hariman and Lucaites's idea of technological reproduction as a means of obtaining iconicity via appropriations and their idea of the social role of photojournalism in dialogue with Mirzoeff's space of appearance, I explore why images of people raising their hands in protest are not considered icons in the general sense but how these may nevertheless challenge iconicity by appropriating embodied political acts. I take the raised hands imagery to connote an embodied gesture, whereas the lone figure standoff is a visual gesture. This distinction will become clear in the analysis below.

The repeated embodied and visual gestures of raised hands and the individual person facing weaponised police call for reflection. In Hariman and Lucaites's depoliticised conceptualisation, the issue of hierarchised humanity is left unexplored. But the particular kind of both embodied and visual repetition of the gestures may be what makes this imagery significant because it draws upon a collective and embodied memory – and perhaps of something that never happened to the viewer or audience – rather than a mythological and impersonal memory detached from the represented individuals and their specific circumstances (Mortensen 2017, 5).

Individual Person Confronting Police

From the many demonstrations and protests following the death of Trayvon Martin in 2012 and in particular Michael Brown in 2014, photographs – often taken by professional photographers and distributed in mainstream media – of protesting masses or individuals have been produced and circulated online as well as in print. The two representations on which I focus in this chapter are not individual images that somehow gained particular resonance. They are instead particular gestures that are themselves appropriations or that have been subsequently appropriated. The first gesture is that of an individual facing police in heavy armour and weaponry.

An example of this kind of projection is the image taken by photographer Jeff Robertson for the Associated Press of a man in a bright blue T-shirt and a cap, with a backpack over his shoulder, being confronted by what appears to be a SWAT team of militarised police. The police are wearing gasmasks and camouflage gear and are pointing their guns at the man, who is facing them with his hands raised in surrender. The photograph was taken during a protest in St. Louis in August 2014. Similarly, a photograph taken two years later by Jonathan Bachman in Baton Rouge in July 2016 shows a woman standing seemingly quietly in the middle of the street as militarised police storm towards her. The excessiveness of the police officers' military outfits contrasts with the tranquillity and everyday-ness of the two black individuals confronting them. Many other images of the same composition have appeared before and since these two mentioned here, and there is good reason to believe that more will appear along the way because the images are immediately recognisable and relatable to the viewer. I argue that this is so because they mimic the iconic photograph of the lone protester facing tanks in Tiananmen Square 1989.

In an illuminating analysis by Hariman and Lucaites (2007, 208–42), the photograph of a lone Chinese protester facing a row of tanks on Tiananmen Square in 1989 is shown to advocate liberalism as the dominant social order and in turn promote consumerism in favour of citizenship. While the photo, versions of which were taken by several photographers, has been known to draw upon semiotic codes connoting the individual against the system and human vulnerability against mechanic militarism and has been seen as a critique of authoritarian regimes, Hariman and Lucaites also show that the perspective and framing of the photo point to a universalisation of the conflict. They argue that the long distance between the object of the photo and the photographer as well as the directional lines on the otherwise empty street adhere to codes of modern political order and the surveillance and disciplining of modern liberalism. The image thus universalises the particular Chinese conflict and elevates its meaning to a call for Western liberal ideals and democracy, based on freedom of the individual and rational deliberation. To Western eyes, liberalism is based on the freedom to choose and pursue one's dreams through consumption. This is why Hariman and Lucaites ultimately see the photo as a sign of Western liberalism's and consumerism's global dominance. Because Western liberalism understands social and political progress as developing through stages leading towards the final stage, occupied by Western states, China's struggle in this case is seen as representing Western political past, pointing towards China's future, which is understood to be modelled after the West. This is not to argue, Hariman and Lucaites assert, that the general meanings of dissent and democracy are not present in the photo. However, Hariman and Lucaites's reading sheds light on the mythology of Western public culture and show how easily we are persuaded of the common sense of liberal democracy and with it the propriety of the modern public sphere. A reading of dissent and democracy cannot stand alone but is intertwined with the mythology of public culture and visuality.

Like the man and the tanks in Tiananmen Square, the photos of the Black Lives Matter protesters are framed to show them standing alone facing excessive military power towards which they appear passive and to which they must eventually surrender. They too draw upon the social and semiotic codes of the individual against the system. They show the individual standing up to the system and encourage the viewer to feel the power of the people inherent in the composition and frame. If the man in Tiananmen Square needed to be viewed from a distance to allow Western viewers a gaze of surveillance that enabled them to mirror their own ideology of modernism in the image, no such need is necessary when it comes to the photograph of Black Lives Matter protesters. They are already part of Western liberal democracy. The Black Lives Matter protest photo does not show the future of another political culture but instead the past within the United States present; the lack of progress and equity when it comes to the racial, hierarchical system. The photos are taken from street level and clearly show the particularity of the people standing up to the police. While the Chinese protester was shown from afar and from behind, excluding any significant markers that could identify details about him, the clothing, hairstyles and political and social markers of the Black Lives Matter protesters are clearly visible. The woman facing the police, for instance, was identified as Ieshia Evans, who placed herself in harm's way because she had had enough: 'People call us African Americans. But really we are Africans living in America. How can we call ourselves Americans when what is supposed to be our national constitution did not recognise us as human beings? We were not people – we were property. And despite the amendments, things have not really changed', she wrote in a comment in *The Guardian* (Evans 2016). Evans stood up in order to question the racial structures and system that underlie Western liberal democracy and that continue to categorise some as more human than others. Like Jackson, Evans questions the meaningfulness of a Constitution that is not upheld for all the people. She highlights the particular experience of African Americans and speaks her mind in a global newspaper following the initial attention, which she prompted through her gesture before the police. The Chinese protester had no way of standing up to the Western liberal media and telling his version of the struggle in China. His photo was thus easily appropriated by the mythology of Western liberal modernism. The question is whether it is necessary for Evans's photo to be read alongside her words and with the gesture of specific experience in order for the image to serve as a political act that creates a space of appearance. Calling the photo of Evans iconic may point to the fact that the photo is seen as part of a general struggle for liberty because of its loyal echoing of Tiananmen Square. As such, Evans was appropriating the iconicity of the Tiananmen Square photo rather than rupturing the participatory public space. However, the repetition of the iconic composition may also be understood as a means of bringing attention to the failure of the liberal modernist reading of that iconic photo. Taking a familiar stand, but with a difference, may shed light on the flaws of universalism and abstract politics (Mirzoeff 2017b).

Hands Up, Don't Shoot

One of the most recognisable representations from the Black Lives Matter movement is the repeated gesture of two raised hands, often accompanied by placards stating 'Hands up, don't shoot'. The gesture and saying have been performed at demonstrations, at football games, at concerts, in Congress by members of the Congressional Black Caucus, and at Brown's funeral. They are a re-enactment of the final moments of the black teen Michael Brown's life before he was shot and killed by officer Darren Wilson in August 2014. Whether the words and the gesture were actually stated and performed by Brown himself has been debated, most notably as part of the case against Wilson. During the trial, it was made clear that due to his gunshot wounds, Brown would have had difficulty raising both hands. Absurdly, this fact was used to discredit witness statements to the point that Brown had surrendered before he was shot (Mirzoeff 2017a). However, more important than the accuracy of Brown's last words and movements is the fact that the re-enactment of the perceived gesture became an embodied icon, reappropriated by different bodies (football players, politicians, activists) and at different venues (stadiums, Congress, the streets) but with a common political claim: defiance against police brutality, particularly that aimed at black bodies.

Raising one's hands in surrender and re-enacting Brown's gesture is thus to be understood as reclaiming the gesture as a political act and rights claim, forging a space of appearance. While the performance may also be seen as a passive and even submissive gesture, playing into the hands of liberal, white America's stereotypes of African Americans (Apel 2014), remaining passive may moreover highlight the excessive force with which passivity is met by law enforcement. The re-enacted gesture of raising their hands and reproducing this gesture in digital imagery both reproduce and reclaim African American history and memory. The re-enactment mimics gestures of surrender while protesting injustice, and this double meaning produces ambivalence, difference or an 'inappropriateness' that ruptures the discourse or habitus of American public life and self-understanding. The images almost mock the power differentials between white and black in the United States by using a gesture of surrender (Bhabha 1994, 85–93). 'Hands up, don't shoot' may in this light be seen as a 'mode of critically evaluating the past as a means of forging identity and organising for future struggles that lies outside of the formal disciplines of history' (Raiford 2011, 212).

Clearly, the gesture is far from simple in its expression and interpretation, and the many points of contestation and deconstruction – from the trial documents to liberal guilt (Apel 2014, Berger 2011) – underscore the fact that the gesture cannot be viewed as iconic. This is not because it lacks aesthetic familiarity, civic performance, semiotic simplicity, emotionality or conflict but for two main reasons: First, the iconic elements are derived from black perspectives. Unlike the impersonal characteristic of mainstream (read: white) iconicity, 'hands up, don't shoot' draws upon semiotic codes readily recognisable to African Americans, who have knowledge or experience of police violence and gun deaths among African American men in particular. The display of simultaneous vulnerability and protest embedded in the gesture mirrors the precariousness of African American lives. The civic performance in the gesture cannot reproduce the public sphere and ideal of the common good because it brings another perspective to the table, a perspective that points towards the difference within the public and the inappropriateness that has been bracketed off in order to sustain the ideal of the common good. The gesture is not an appropriation but an original political act that disrupts the visual public sphere by mimicking and mocking the differentials and injustices of US racial politics. Second, its iconicity is embodied rather than visual. 'Hands up, don't shoot' is a physical act, which is reproduced and appropriated, reclaiming 'the right to existence' (Mirzoeff 2017a, 100). By repeating Michael Brown's gesture, the protesters embody – rather than represent – the rights claim. Nevertheless, the gesture is distributed and circulated visually through digital media and platforms, constituting a spontaneous meme that initiated an interaction between direct action and digital media and provided protesters with a new self-image (Mirzoeff 2015, 297). Mirzoeff identifies this interaction as a new modality of visual culture that allows it to generate visual activist projects – visual political acts.

'Hands up, don't shoot' not only shows us opportunities for participating in public by reappropriating the original embodied icon through similarly embodied repetitions of the gesture rather than through digital decontextualisation and recontextualisation (as was also the case in the analysis of the individual person confronting police). The gesture also challenges the ideal of iconicity by growing from an embodied and situated reality, thereby creating political acts. This means that both the original act and its appropriations are embodied as well as digitally networked and archived. This furthermore sheds light on the importance of the sexualised, racialised and naturalised body that may comprise the act or perform the appropriations. By insisting upon the embodied action, 'hands up, don't shoot' poses the question of who counts as human – the vulnerable, protesting body or the impersonal character of universal whiteness. 'Hands up, don't shoot' is an arresting gesture, which – like a photograph – pauses action for perpetuity in order to allow us to reflect upon that which follows. Unlike a photograph, 'the action prevents the media from its usual call for closure, healing, and moving on', argues Mirzoeff (2017a, 103). Continual re-enactments serve as reminders of the ruptures and encourage new perspectives on police violence and the prison industrial complex.

VERNACULAR EXPRESSIONS: CITIZEN MEDIA EXPRESSIONS

In the above analyses, I have sought to draw out structural similarities between my conceptualisation of citizen journalism and Mirzoeff's space of appearance as well as between the public sphere and iconicity as conceptualised by Hariman and Lucaites. I argue that citizen journalism must be understood as an embodied, political and situated act if we are to take seriously the materiality of the citizen and her position of expression. The practice of citizen journalism, then, produces citizen subjects. Just as iconic photojournalism cannot allow for specific, grounded imagery but continuously reproduces imagery based on the insistence of the universality and mythology of whiteness and liberal democracy in a Western context, the public sphere is regulated in favour of the common good and the idealised frame of deliberative democracy. These structural similarities are detectable because contemporary expressions from citizens take vernacular and creative forms that become visible by bouncing off the backdrop of 'commonsense' visuality. The structures are moreover similar because of their relationship to temporality. Whereas iconicity and the public sphere are built upon reproduction of the same or appropriations to challenge the same, the space of appearance and citizen journalism grow from embodied experience and counter-memories.

The point about archivization made in chapter 4 (that it produces subjectivity through re-membering the past while pointing towards the future) becomes relevant here again. On the one hand, when Jackson used the text 'Laws Used for Regulating the Conduct of Slaves' to underscore the labourers' plight and their right to better wages and working conditions, he remembered the text and the times in which it had taken effect, yet he did so while emphasising the changed power relationship. This kind of rearranging of the meaning of the historical text created a space in which Jackson's rights claim appeared. The Declaration of Independence, on the other hand, is an iconic text. It was not just the fact that Jackson did not recognise from experience the ideal claims made in the text but also that his role and the role of *The Herald* within the space generated by the iconic Constitutional text demanded participation within the already-given framework. The first text, then, called upon an embodied and political memory, while the second demanded universal and impersonal participation. However, identifying the preconditions for and components of a space of appearance or citizen journalism is an empirical task, requiring careful attention and analysis. Here, I reintroduce Gilroy's ideas of vernacular expressions and the changing same in order to think of the space of appearance and citizen journalism not as structurally similar but as empirically interchangeable in contemporary digital and non-digital expressions.

Vernacular expressions are expressions not regulated by formal speech or writing but formulated on the basis of inborn structures and qualities. Rather than following a melancholic trajectory leading back to a lost past, Gilroy uses the example of music as a mnemonic device that rearranges the concept of tradition into a changing same, practiced through vernacular expressions such as music and in the culture surrounding the African American music scene (Gilroy 1993, 198). Gilroy aims to understand African American cultural expressions not as essence but as subjectivity formation. He finds that discussions about authenticity versus artifice miss the mark and miss the opportunity to shift perspectives from a binary to a dynamic understanding of cultural politics (Gilroy 1991). For Gilroy, African American music does not refer to an unproblematic historical or traditional past that must be bypassed in order for true, authentic African American expression to emerge. Instead, it is the subtle changes that invoke tradition through disruptions and breaks, which respond to 'the destabilizing flux of the postcontemporary world' (126). It is, in other words, the process of archivization in fractal form that produces the changing same of 'tradition' or historicity. The difference between appropriations, theorised in relation to iconic imagery, and the changing same lies in their genealogies.

Whereas appropriations demand a recognisable same to politically or satirically appropriate, the changing same is based upon counter-imagery or counter-music functioning as mnemonic devices.

To summarise, I wish to show the extent to which this vernacular expression, these spaces of appearance and these practices of citizen journalism challenge modern memory and public space. I have already introduced images and music as possible citizen journalistic modalities, and it does not end there. Other practices include street performance, street art and graffiti, demonstrations, flash-mobs, the creation of shared communication platforms, blogs, translations, mockumentaries, archiving, modifications of video games and the creation of fan art to raise awareness of political agendas (Baker and Blaagaard 2016, 1–2). These varied and creative citizen media practices risk being appropriated and co-opted by corporate culture and fed back into mainstream expressions, just as Jackson wished for his journalism to become a public voice for all of St. Croix. However, if politically embodied or intentional, they are produced as political acts claiming a space or a right to appear on their own terms. They are produced from and produce in their practitioners and audiences '[t]hat common sensation [that] occurs when we see, in the sense of coming to understand, a photograph *of* the space of appearance that emanates *from* the space of appearance, contains its potential and is not simply *about* it (as in the form of photojournalism)' (Mirzoeff 2017a).

Marwan M. Kraidy (2016, 5–6) makes a similar connection between embodiment and political subversiveness in his brilliant book *The Naked Blogger of Cairo*. At the heart of the processes that he terms creative insurgency 'is the human body as tool, medium, symbol, and metaphor', while '[r]evolutionaries engage in these physical and symbolic practices to wrench political power from the body of the dictator and birth popular sovereignty'. That is, revolutionaries seek to become citizens through a continuous struggle against the system. In one of his many insightful analyses of revolutionary art during the Egyptian uprising in 2011, Kraidy focusses on the blogger Aliia al-Mahdy and her blog *A Rebel's Diary*, which featured nude self-portraits. Authorship, Marwan asserts, underlies the crucial distinction between the role of the female body as feminist political expression such as that of al-Mahdy and the role of general artistic female nudes: 'Authoring the representation of one's own naked body is important because it proves an ability to convey one's own thoughts, the capacity to represent one's own self, the power to lead one's own life on one's own terms – agency' (166). Al-Mahdy's nude selfies create a space of appearance because they point to a call for political change emanating from that site which needs the change. Al-Mahdy performed visual activism by producing an interaction between 'pixels and actions to make change' (Mirzoeff 2015, 297). Her photos are cultural expressions or forms that invite reflection and action from viewers around the world but particularly in Egypt. This is not to say that contemporary cultural expressions or formats of political acts and subjectivity formations are exclusively digital and visual. At the other end of the spectrum of citizen journalistic expressions is translation. Mona Baker (2016) understands 'translation' in a narrow and a broad sense. Narrowly, translation is used to concretely translate eyewitness or journalistic narratives into different languages in order for the world to understand the extent of revolutions. In a broader sense, translation pertains to all communicators, activists and artists who work to present to a larger, global audience. Rather than understanding translators as skilled service people, Baker urges a redefinition of the relationship between activists and translators which recognises the equally political act of translating.

Citizen journalism is thus both the act and the expression of this act. 'Hands up, don't shoot', African American rap music, graffiti and many other formats of political expression produce political subjectivities and citizens while raising awareness, changing strategies or protesting their particular topics of social and political contestation. Appropriations of mainstream products, images, music and so on may be political but are so in a different manner: Their contestation is always given in relation and close proximity to the political object through which they define their cause. Appropriations are political insofar as they challenge the mainstream or the political same, yet they operate within and on the terms set by the 'theatrical imagination' (Chouliaraki 2013a, 192) or what in chapter 2 I termed the participatory public. It, then, bears repeating that despite Chouliaraki's and others' political aim of urging solidarity and empathetic relations within the theatre of imagination, the field of humanitarianism (from which Chouliaraki's agonistic solidarity emanates) is itself steeped in unequal political relations. The accountability and responsiveness stressed by Chouliaraki is a welcome strategy but must also be understood to be the responsibility of the Western speakers. And even then, the question remains whether the participatory public itself does not require a set of skills, knowledges and reference points in order to engage meaningfully in changing political agendas. Are creative breaks and fractal disruptions without reference to the political same meaningfully received within an agonistic space such as the theatre of imagination or participatory public? The difficulty we face in responding affirmatively to this question should not prevent us from continuing to try to develop creative and affirmative responses.

NOTES

1. See chapter 1, in which Patton's discussion of the Deleuzian event is applied to the colonial situation.
2. See chapter 4.
3. As noted in chapter 4, 3 July is the day of Crucian Emancipation. Jackson's notes on The Declaration of Independence in 1917 were published on 3 July not 4 July. No explanation was given in the editorial.

6

Conclusions

Citizen Journalism as an Act for Transformation

> Recognizing the power of the erotic within our lives can give us the energy to pursue genuine change within our world, rather than merely settling for a shift of characters in the same weary drama.
>
> —Audre Lorde, 'Uses of the Erotic', 59

The passionate words of the eminent African American scholar and poet Audre Lorde resonate across time and strike a relevant note about political change and civic responsibility, which are also my main concerns here. In this book, I have sought to construct a multilayered argument for a diversified set of interlocutors, spread across a number of discrete but interrelated fields. I have aimed to shift the perspective on citizen journalism by insisting upon its political roots and implications. In so doing, I have broadened the definition of political practice so as to underscore its importance for citizenship. As a result, the citizen is both deconstructed and reaffirmed as an active formation of subjectivity. But the deconstruction of the citizen has not left the political unchanged either: I have argued that the political stems from an embodied and situated experience, which is necessarily diversified even if it is shared by multiple subjects and is by definition collective. I understand 'community' not as a homogeneous entity bonded by presumed commonalities but rather as a heterogeneous assemblage that draws its power from the differences among its multiple members. Being situated and embodied, the plurality of these differences acts as an aggregating factor, not as a cause of disaggregation. While embodied experience may be perceived as too personal and subjective to successfully engage in and change political publics, I have argued that it is the common denominator of all such publics, stressing that it is the interdependence between different but situated people that carries the thrust of political activism, movement and change. The embodiedness and situatedness of each and every subject produce a creative and affirmative bond between them which respects differential positions and power differentials but avoids dialectical oppositions. Becoming-subjects is, then, a matter not of mere personal vicissitudes but instead of subjectivity formations – formations of the relational embodied and situated self – forging a communal space of the political.

Audre Lorde pointed to such a radical shift within the scholarly field of antiracist feminist theory many years ago when she spoke of the power of the erotic – 'the lifeforce of women; of that creative energy empowered, the knowledge and use of which we are now reclaiming our language, our history, our dancing, our loving, our work, our lives' (Lorde 2007 [1978], 55) – as the starting point for political intervention and change. Her famous statement: 'The master's tools will never dismantle the master's house' (Lorde 2007 [1979], 110–13) was a call for this radical change in perspective, language and voice, because simply allowing more voices access and listening to them within the same dreary drama (2007 [1978], 59) does not alter the structure of oppression of those voices. If people in an underdog position are listened to and heard within the participatory public today, it is because their voices are able to beat the modern master at his own game, yet they will never generate real and profound change (2007 [1979], 112). By extension, this indicates that new formats are necessary for new content to emerge. Moreover, formats of expression and political content may be interlocked so that the tenor and rhythm of a voice or a newspaper breaking the monopoly of state-sanctioned editorial boards in a colonial community create a space and a voice simultaneously. Based on this book's analyses and theoretical discussions, this is the kind of process for which I wish to reserve the term 'citizen journalism'.

In this concluding chapter, I draw together the threads of arguments that run through the book as well as answer some remaining questions. I begin by revisiting the radicality of Braidotti's concepts of becoming-minoritarian and the politics of location, which have been guiding principles of different modalities throughout the book. I elaborate upon the political and ethical implications of these concepts, particularly as they pertain to the relationship between subjectivity formations and citizen journalism. I do this in the 'Becoming Citizen Subjectivity' section. In the 'Postcolonial Citizen Journalism' section, I continue by investigating why citizen journalism – in the terms laid out in the book and in the preceding section in particular – is a postcolonial issue. I do so by drawing together the theories of poststructuralist and postcolonial thought about the citizen and bringing them to bear on the practice of citizen journalism that this book has developed. Finally, in the 'The Stakes of Shifting Perspectives' section, I explore the political and ethical implications of the new perspective on citizen journalism. Here, I seek tentative conclusions relating to three questions introduced in chapter 1: How does citizen journalism engage with the question of who counts as human – that is, who is able to appear on his or her own terms? How may citizen journalism be conceptualised as a political act that forges a space of appearance and potential subjectivity formation? And finally, if citizen journalism visually and linguistically acts upon the world by forging such a space, to what extent does that change the public spaces and concepts of citizenship and civil rights?

BECOMING CITIZEN SUBJECTIVITY

If citizen journalism aims to change society, then what distinguishes citizen journalism from other forms of political action, such as activism and social movements? Understanding citizen journalism as conceptual practice means that citizen journalism can be distinguished from activism and social movements on the level of the very definition of the citizen, who has been conceptualised as a process of subjectivity formation or becoming, and on the level of journalism, which is redefined as creative events of communication that address a public. Citizen journalism is a process of becoming citizen – that is, politically engaged and invested through the creative force of expression. Citizen journalism functions on a deeply personal and affective level while acknowledging that the individual is always already enmeshed in a wider language, history, politics and life. It follows that the journalism practiced by citizen journalists potentially takes different shapes than does traditional journalism (although many different formats are possible in traditional journalism). This means that while activism and social movements may be seen as political acts similar to the political acts of citizen journalism discussed in chapter 2, they focus first and foremost on a common cause rather than on the political subjectivity of the people and communities acting and their interdependence with their surroundings. Citizen journalism is an embodied political act and the expression of the act, which in turn produces subjectivity and a public. Second, citizen journalism shatters the participatory public's format and insists upon a new language. Citizen journalism is thus a critical and creative force that does not simply aspire to being heard but that requires the listener to educate herself. Listening is a privilege, and the ability to shift perspectives is a process that demands that this privilege be recognised and accounted for – like shedding old skin – if one is to learn and unlearn old practices of power hierarchies.

This latter point builds upon Audre Lorde's reproach of white feminist theorists for using the hierarchical building blocks and social architectural structures of the patriarchy to inform their conferences and summits. Often, Lorde (2007 [1979], 113) argues, women have been charged with the responsibility of educating men on the strengths and needs of women: As a result, the patriarchy keeps women occupied with men's concerns. Similarly, African American women are now being tasked with educating white women on the particularities of African American experience, while being underrepresented and silenced on other issues. In this manner, feminist theory reproduces patriarchal structures of oppression while seeking to dismantle them. Taking my cue from Lorde, I argue that simply learning to listen – that is, inviting subaltern or other(ed) voices to participate in the already-established (modern) public – is not enough, because it continues to ask the outsider to relate to the already-established public, casting her as not-modern or somehow an uneasy fit with modernity and its concomitant structures. Although the move to encompass more voices recognises the lack of diversity within the public, it expects representatives of diversity to adhere to certain formats of expression that may limit what can be heard. Instead, listening needs to be a process of both allowing new content and new forms to emerge outside the participatory public if necessary, while nevertheless taking into account the subaltern or other(ed) position as outsider. That is, listening needs to be a process of simultaneously learning and unlearning practices in which a space of appearance occurs. Engaging with the space of appearance does not mean that other areas are occluded and pushed out; instead, the space of public engagement and the political is expanded. Remaining outside of mainstream public participation is paramount to the expression of citizen journalism, although the outsider position may simply be slightly different from sameness: for instance, a traditional newspaper that speaks from and of a new people; a nationally televised news show that satirises and mocks – rather than reports – the news; or a gesture that redefines and re-members political acts. The colonial discursive strategy of mimicry based upon ambivalence and slippages (Bhabha 1994, 85–93) is reproduced as strategies of resistance against the logic of modernity.

Recognising and unlearning privilege in order to creatively expand the political space requires a practice of accounting for the self. This is what Adrienne Rich and Rosi Braidotti call a politics of location and becoming-minoritarian. Rich's and Braidotti's calls for a politics of location propose a knowledge production growing from citizens' embodied subjectivity. This produced knowledge in turn allows for new meaning-making processes that challenge status quo and common sense knowledge. Common sense is often built upon long-established truths that are not assessed or challenged but have instead been institutionalised. New perspectives may change this and present another understanding of, for instance, history or gendered and racial experiences. This is not an argument for a relativism in which each person holds her own version of the truth equal to that of another. It is a matter of multiple and intermingled strands of understandings and experiences combining to give a fuller account of the rhizomatic network of interrelations that make up society and subjects. Becoming-minoritarian is the ethical response to this social analysis. It is about consciously and conscientiously accounting for one's own constantly shifting and vibrating position and relationship – be it of power or of subservience – as a process of becoming. Becoming-minoritarian is a process of expression (Braidotti 2011, 151) that eclectically assembles creativity and intensities. It is integrally connected to the outside – that is, to others (153), but does not adhere to a powerful institution. Becoming-minoritarian is thus fundamental to processes of deterritorialization because it uproots and unsettles power structures, such as the logic of modernity or racial and gendered hierarchies.

Whereas traditional journalism as well as studies conducted in the field take a starting point in the institutionalisation and societal importance of journalistic practices, I have argued that citizen journalism must be seen as a process of becoming – that is, it must emerge from an underdog or outsider position and must call into being a public that is held accountable and required to engage in a similar process of becoming. The cartographic reading of *The Herald* shows us that citizen journalism is created in a swirl of historical, geopolitical, racial and cultural movements that influence and form the embodied subjectivities of Jackson and his contemporaries. The analyses of imagery of the Black Lives Matter movement likewise simultaneously draw upon critical and embodied memory and ambivalences. These movements moreover tear at the narrative and memory of colonial history and working relations, destabilising the master narrative and establishing a counter-memory. Knowledge production emanating from a process of becoming challenges the status quo by presenting a host of alternatives and interdependencies that make us see and understand differently. Obviously, traditional journalism also challenges the status quo, but it does so from a position of institutionalised power that accompanies the professional journalistic practice and with an aim of reterritorializing and stabilising the previous or a similar order. Citizen journalism does not have an aim or endpoint but is instead a continued struggle and opening up of identifications and interrelations.

The relationship between space and time – the former in terms of colonial possessions and positions, national boundaries and cosmopolitan connections and the latter in terms of memory, counter-memory, historicity and the future – are important axes for the colonial case, but they are moreover relevant for presenting the case for citizen journalism in digitalised space. First, in terms of spatiality in digitalised political engagements, it is clear that digital space stretches as far as energy resources and economies allow. A recent example of digital citizen journalism is, as discussed in the previous chapter, Black Lives Matter, a civil rights movement fighting for racial equality and justice. It was conceived in the United States as a protest against the innumerable deaths of young black men at the hands of white police officers. In the online world, Black Lives Matter is a point of connection in Europe and the United Kingdom as well. The movement is moreover visible through the #BLM hashtag, yet physical protest and engagement are important aspects of the movement's platform and ideology.[1]

The #metoo hashtag activism,[2] which is a movement that highlights the extent of public sexual abuse of women, is another example of digital citizen journalism. The hashtag follows up on several ongoing legal claims of abuse suffered by women at the hands of powerful executives and celebrities in the creative industries as well as in political parties and administrations. However, the hashtag goes beyond these claims by following women's statements and stories about everyday sexism, extreme abuse and even rape. The movement may also be said to continue a budding resistance against the 2016 general election in the United States, in which Donald J. Trump was elected president of the United States despite numerous allegations of sexual abuse as well as the so-called 'Hollywood Access' tape, in which Trump bragged about sexually harassing women. In the wake of the election, Braidotti (2016) called for organised resistance by philosophers and activists alike, calling upon the 'multitude of "bad girls" aspiring to self-determination, capable of triggering new social imaginaries and igniting unexpected political passions'. The #metoo movement may be the modality of expression favoured by a selection of 'bad girls'.

The #metoo campaign is arguably citizen journalism in the sense discussed and developed in this book due to its embodied and situated vision of social change. Each testimony of abuse is another relation in the asymmetrical web of witnesses pushing and prodding against the common sense of female silence and subservience to power. It is a different format than journalism, certainly, and it is different because the digital expression is part of the message and the change it pursues: that singular events in concert drive a shift in perspectives. The world seen through female eyes appears through the tapestry of testimonies and occurrences of witnessing. The 'metoo' hashtag is being used across the Western mediascape: Like Black Lives Matter, it originated in the United States, but its political force is not contained within national boundaries.[3] Both hashtags and protest movements take a perspective from the outside, forging a new political space. Both are expressions that are being challenged, particularly in order to reterritorialize and stabilise the former order. Backlashes such as All Lives Matter responses to Black Lives Matter and attempts at slandering female witnesses[4] who speak of their abuse are all part of the impact made by these movements. Second, in terms of time, digital citizen journalism is grounded in memory and uprisings against oppression. In relation to #metoo, the case of Anita Hill, an attorney and academic who in 1991 accused then-nominee to the US Supreme Court Clarence Thomas of sexual harassment, is a historical point of reference. Although Thomas was still confirmed for the Supreme Court, the case changed legal practices concerning sexual harassment in US workplaces. Other online projects, such as the Everyday Sexism project,[5] also serve as precursors and enablers of #metoo.

The digital space functions as an archive that reaches into the future. Using the hashtag in Twitter-generated tweets or on other digital platforms enables other users to search and find related stories online. The hashtag is an archivization mechanism that – instead of being a nationally structured and policed selection – leaves it up to content creators to tag and store their product, their tweets. It remains to be seen, however, whether this renders history more inclusive. Unlike the microfilm archives of *The Herald*, the digital archive has yet to reveal its meaning-making abilities and importance for subjectivity formations.

Black Lives Matter and #metoo are processes of becoming that both generate knowledge through new content and expression and call upon a public to account for itself, its privileges and its positions. It is an integral process that does not assume a distinction between the process of producing and the process of consuming citizen journalism, not because the users are now producers or prosumers, but because they are based in processes of subjectivity formations that moreover extend beyond the subject.

POSTCOLONIAL CITIZEN JOURNALISM

Citizen journalism is built upon the interdependency of subjects engaging in the process. Like the contemporary examples of Black Lives Matter and #metoo, Jackson and *The Herald* encompassed readers in the processes of becoming citizens in a (post)colonial space. Despite the obvious example of digital webs criss-crossing geographical space, in this book I have taken a starting point in a historical, colonial case in order to formulate the political concepts embedded in citizen journalism. The analyses have shown how the postcolonial case of *The Herald* both draws attention to the limits of the participatory public and suggests a different conceptualisation of the cosmopolitan, global reach of citizen journalism. In this section, I discuss why I think citizen journalism is a postcolonial issue.

In chapter 1, I argued that the poststructuralist theories of conceptual practice and becoming-minoritarian have more in common with postcolonial theories than is often acknowledged in the scholarship. Fleshing out the dynamics of the process of becoming-minoritarian in the section above, it is clear, however, that this is a rhizomatic process of singular becomings that appear differently according to subjects' position and privilege. A white man may have a different perspective and a different reaction to injustice than a black woman due to differences in their life experiences and collective memories. But their gender and racial markers may not be the crucial differences between their understandings. Affluence, professional trade, geographical belonging, personal experience and political affiliation may all hold important clues to a subject's technologies of the self and underscore her accountability of location. No one should live 'on external directives' and 'outside ourselves' (Lorde 2007 [1978], 58), defined by our racial, sexual, gendered and class-related markers; everyone must instead live outward from within while recognising and being accountable to our difference. In this manner, 'our acts against oppression become integral with self, motivated and empowered from within' (58). In the words of Braidotti (2006b, 201), 'affirmation, the result of a process of transformation of negative into positive passions, is essentially and intrinsically the expression of joy and positivity. This is constitutive of the *potentia* of the subject'. The erotic or the affirmative potentia of the subject is expressed through the process of becoming, which in this book is understood as key to the conceptualisation of citizen journalism.

Although becoming-minoritarian is embedded in a postcolonial and imperial world in which a particular power relation and distribution of privilege may be presumed, it is in the hybrid or Third Space of negotiating meaning (Bhabha 1994, 36–37) that the political act emerges. 'It is in the emergence of the interstices – the overlap and displacement of domains of difference – that the intersubjective and collective experiences of *nationess*, community interest, or cultural value are negotiated' (2). In the following, then, I first revisit becoming-minoritarian as a process of change embedded in postcolonial politics and history. In order to do so, I briefly refer to theories that recognise the affinities between postcolonial theories and poststructuralist theories, such as Homi Bhabha's early work on culture and Gilroy's creative incorporation of Deleuze into his postcolonial thinking. Second, I explore the limits of the participatory public made visible through the postcolonial perspective and argue that citizen journalism is a postcolonial issue.

As discussed in chapter 4, Gilroy understands the African American experience as a counter-position to the representational figure of black iconicity that has been used as a sign for the oppressed and irrational. Gilroy (1994) proposes an alternative, contextual figuration, the Black Atlantic, which is a means of understanding identity formations and political acts that may stem from diasporic communities on both sides of the Atlantic. Following a rhizomatic (non-unified, non-centric) structure, Gilroy argues for more inclusive and open-ended thinking about the relationship between African diasporic communities and European modernity – two themes he finds to have been kept apart artificially in cultural and philosophical thought. The figure of the Black Atlantic aims to bring together the two themes, and Gilroy thereby draws upon the trope of ships at sea, alluding both to slave trade and to the movements of thinkers of African descent occurring during those travels. Echoing Edward Said's sentiment that 'cultures are too intermingled, their contents and histories too interdependent and hybrid, for surgical separation into large and mostly ideological oppositions like Orient and Occident' (Said 1994, xii), Gilroy reminds us that American and Caribbean people of African descent have throughout black intellectual history travelled to Europe as well as to Africa, producing insights not exclusively developed from within a cordoned-off black experience, albeit from an affirmative and passionate self. This approach is distinctly poststructuralist if not Deleuzian. It speaks to the hybridity of Bhabha's Third Space as well as to the importance of self and subjectivity formations.

Through extensive analyses in *The Location of Culture*, Bhabha (1994, 175) perceives poststructuralist theory from a position of postcolonial contra-modernity and uses it to deconstruct – pointing to the impossibility of – the West's determination of colonisation. Like Gilroy, Bhabha insists that the defining power lies in the perspective from outside and the inescapable nuances and richness of that position. Bhabha (178–79) identifies in poststructuralist thinking an understanding of an 'enunciative present as a liberatory discursive strategy', which is beyond binary positions, oppressions and identity politics. These strategies in turn become a way to open up a new space for identifications. In his writing and analyses, Bhabha (185) identifies practices of mimicry, hybridity and sly civility to express the 'subversive strategy of subaltern agency that negotiates its own authority through a process of iterative "unpicking" and incommensurable, insurgent relinking'. These practices of time lag involve 'conceiving of the time of political action and understanding as opening up a space that can accept and regulate the differential structure of the moment of intervention without rushing to produce a unity of the social antagonism or contradiction' (25). In other words, these are practices that challenge the structure and logic of modernity and insist on its own space of appearance, which in turn does not reterritorialize. The similarity to Gilroy's figuration of the Black Atlantic – a fluid and encompassing space – is clear.

Both Bhabha and Gilroy use the colonial experience to question modernity as well as the concomitant concept of the nation-state, and they strive to produce space for new formats and senses. It is the postcolonial critique that creates the foundation for a marginal voice or an outsider position that does not aspire to become part of the centre but that shifts the focus and subverts the conversation by calling upon a public. Bhabha's and Gilroy's thinking requires a reconsideration of the concept of the citizen and the intersubjective relationships that make up communities that transcend national boundaries. In chapter 2, using theorists such as Isin and Balibar, I argued for a similar process in order to capture the idea of the citizen of citizen journalism. I used Isin and Nielsen's (2008) ideas of political acts of citizenship to deconstruct the concept of the citizen and develop an idea of the citizen as a process that disrupts the national frame of reference in journalism and conventions upheld by the public sphere. The colonial case of *The Herald* illustrates the postcolonial and outsider position as fundamental to becoming citizen and to creating citizen journalism, presenting us with an analytical starting point in colonial history and geography. This insistence on a colonial case not only challenges the centrality of the nation-state for journalism and political engagement but also releases us from the digital saturation of the debates on citizen journalism and the particular kind of democratisation suggested through digital media debates. The case invites a counter-reading of both journalism history and Danish (colonial) history. Besides critiquing modernity, the postcolonial starting point creates an alternative cartography, which clarifies the significance and particularity of today's citizen journalistic expressions, both in terms of content (against oppression of and for oppressed people) and format (disruptive and rhizomatic). My geographical, embodied and political starting point is fundamental to my theoretical and conceptual understanding.

Citizen journalism is a postcolonial issue because the outsider position out of which and for which citizen journalism is produced is grounded in colonial differentiations based on racial and sexual differences. It is, moreover, a postcolonial issue because it questions the concept of the nation-state as a dominant frame of reference in political engagements and historical narratives.

THE STAKES OF SHIFTING PERSPECTIVES

It could reasonably be asked: Why retain the term 'citizen journalism' when the meaning of the term in this book has become so far removed from the original use? This book has proposed a shift in perspective from the more traditional and journalistic perception of the term, which understands citizen journalism as challenging – if not oppositional to – traditional or professional journalism. I have argued that the citizen is not simply a user or producer participating in the journalistically defined participatory public or public sphere but instead a subjectivity-creating process that produces other publics and potentially social change through political acts of expression. Because these other publics are defined through address as well as across bridges between geographically detached locations, journalism is no longer conceptualised as a nation-building reproduction of the same but instead as creative events that connect and develop social and political communities of selves. Granted, an alternative term to 'citizen journalism' could be 'subjectivity-formative events'. But perhaps for obvious linguistic and semantic reasons and because a shift in perspective is always more easily identifiable if the position from which that shift moves or to which it relates is visible, I have chosen to take my starting point in the already recognisable concept of citizen journalism in order to argue for a rereading of the term. However, my understanding of the practice of citizen journalism differs radically from how the concept is understood in media and journalism studies more broadly; moreover, I focus less on the practicalities of writing and creating citizen journalism than on that which citizen journalism produces – that is, subjectivity formations through political acts. I have sought to consider citizen journalism as a conceptual practice that produces a certain kind of understanding of the citizen and of journalism but more importantly that potentially produces a different kind of society.

As a conceptual practice, citizen journalism also embodies questions regarding the kinds of social and ethical relations and materialities that are produced. Citizen journalism as an act for transformation sheds new light on political engagement and mobilisation for change by subjects through the media. It therefore becomes necessary to seek answers – if only tentative ones – to the questions of what citizen journalism tells us about who counts as a citizen and as human in contemporary society. In this book, I have followed Nancy Fraser's critique of the public sphere and liberal democracy's tendency to favour the already-agreed-upon and common sense. That is, Fraser argues that while consensus is supposedly reached through debate and deliberation in the Habermasian public sphere, the topics relevant for discussion are defined through previous debates and consensus. Introduction of new topics relevant to marginalised peoples and outsiders is all but impossible. Marginalised positions within the public sphere are not considered but are overlooked in the name of equality. Arguing for a more inclusive public sphere in which the margins are invited to speak and the centre is inclined to listen is admirable and necessary. However, I have sought to show that this is not enough if we wish to break the frame in which the human and grievable lives – as Butler (2009) puts it – are set. If political acts indicate subjects' insistence on existing by disrupting habitus and consensus, then what follows is an insistence on a different concept of the human which is not dependent on differential racial markers, linguistic references and national boundaries but which instead takes to task those colonial and modern logics. It is, furthermore, not the job of the marginalised to ask the centre to listen. It is instead the obligation of whoever holds the central position to educate themselves to understand the significance of the political act. Citizen journalism could be a means of conceptualising the process of the political act, which allows the formerly marginalised to appear on their own terms. As such, citizen journalism could be conceptualised as a political act that forges a space of appearance and potential subjectivity formation. However, examples of citizen voices breaking the mould and the frames are few and far between.

If citizen journalism acts upon the world – visually and linguistically – by forging a space of appearance, by disrupting habitus or discourse, to what extent does this change the public spaces and concepts of citizenship and civil rights? As the above examples of the activism of #metoo and Black Lives Matter as well as the case of *The Herald* show, the movements of de- and reterritorializations are unpredictable and unending. That which is at stake when we shift perspectives, however, is an ability to imagine otherwise. Imagination is linked to memory, and as suggested in chapter 5, we may appropriate the critical memory of the 'Hands up, don't shoot' imagery or follow Braidotti (2006b, 168) in arguing that '[w]hen you remember to become what you are – a subject-in-becoming – you actually reinvent yourself on the basis of what you hope you could become with a little help from your friends'. Indeed, we all have the ethical responsibility to open up and learn from one another. Reconceptualising citizen journalism as subjectivity formation from the outsider position that produces expression of and for the community in which it operates offers us the potential for a political and personal reclaiming of language, history, dancing, loving, working, living (Lorde 2007, 55).

NOTES

1. See https://blacklivesmatter.com/. Accessed 29/11/2017.

2. Writing in late 2017, as the #metoo campaign is gaining momentum, it is difficult to foresee the movement's future. Powerful movements towards reterritorialization and towards undercutting the women who are speaking up against sexual harassment and a culture of oppression are already underway. Whether the movement will change practices or whether old practices will be restored remains to be seen.

3. See http://edition.cnn.com/2016/07/11/europe/black-lives-matter-protests-europe/index.html and http://abcnews.go.com/International/black-lives-matter-protests-global-ireland-south-africa/story?id=40546549. Accessed 29/11/2017.

4. See for instance the case of the right-wing activist, who produced posters claiming actor Meryl Streep was aware of executives' abuse of women but kept silent. The case was covered internationally in major newspapers.

5. See https://everydaysexism.com/. Accessed 29/11/2017.

Bibliography

Agamben, G. (2002). *Remnants of Auschwitz: The Witness and the Archive*. New York: Zone Books.

Allan, S. (2009). 'Histories of citizen journalism'. In S. Allan and E. Thorsen (eds.), *Citizen Journalism: Global Perspectives* (pp. 17–32). New York: Peter Lang.

———. (2011). 'Citizen journalism'. In J. D. H. Downing (ed.), *Encyclopedia of Social Movements* (p. 98). Thousand Oaks, CA: Sage.

———. (2013). *Citizen Witnessing*. New York/London: Routledge.

——— (ed.). (2012). *The Routledge Companion to News and Journalism*. Second edition. New York/London: Routledge.

Allan. S., and E. Thorsen (eds.). (2009). *Citizen Journalism: Global Perspectives*. New York: Peter Lang.

Anderson, B. (1991). *Imagined Communities*. London/New York: Verso.

Apel, D. (2014). *'Hands up, Don't Shoot': Surrendering to Liberal Illusions*. Baltimore: Johns Hopkins University Press.

Arendt, H. (1958). *The Human Condition*. Chicago: University of Chicago Press.

Austin, J. L. (1962). *How to Do Things with Words*. Oxford: Clarendon Press.

Baker, M. (2016). 'Beyond the spectacle: Translation and solidarity in contemporary protest movements'. In M. Baker (ed.), *Translating Dissent: Voices from and with the Egyptian Revolution* (pp. 1–18). London/New York: Routledge.

Baker, M., and B. Blaagaard. (2016). 'Reconceptualizing citizen media: A preliminary charting of a complex domain'. In M. Baker and B. Blaagaard (eds.), *Citizen Media and Public Spaces: Diverse Expressions of Citizenship and Dissent* (pp. 1–22). New York/London: Routledge.

Balibar, E. (1989). 'Citizen subject'. Translated by J. B. Swenson. *Cahiers Confrontations* 20 (Winter): 33–57.

———. (1991). 'The nation form'. In Etienne Balibar and Immanuel Wallerstein (eds.), *Race, Nation, Class: Ambiguous Identities* (pp. 86–106). New York/London: Verso.

———. (2004). *We, the People of Europe?* Translated by J. Swenson. Princeton, NJ: Princeton University Press.

Bastian, J. A. (2003). *Owning Memory. How a Caribbean Community Lost Its Archives and Found Its History*. Westport and London: Libraries Unlimited.
Beckett, C. (2008). *Supermedia: Saving Journalism So It Can Save the World*. Malden, MA/Oxford: Blackwell.
Benhabib, S. et al. (2006). *Another Cosmopolitanism: Hospitality, Sovereignty and Democratic Iterations*. Oxford: Oxford University Press.
Benhabib, S. (2007). 'Twilight of sovereignty or the emergence of cosmopolitan norms? Rethinking citizenship in volatile times'. *Citizenship Studies* 11(1): 19–36.
Berger, M. A. (2011). *Seeing Through Race*. Berkeley: University of California Press.
Bhabha, H. (1994). *The Location of Culture*. New York/London: Routledge.
Bignall, S., and P. Patton. (2010). 'Introduction: Deleuze and the postcolonial: Conversations, negotiations, mediations'. In S. Bignall and P. Patton (eds.), *Deleuze and the Postcolonial* (pp. 1–19). Edinburgh: Edinburgh University Press.
Blaagaard, B. B. (2011). 'Whose freedom? Whose memory? Commemorating Danish colonialism in St. Croix'. *Social Identities* 17(1): 61–72.
———. (2013). 'Situated, embodied, political: Expressions of citizen journalism'. *Journalism Studies* 14(2): 187–200.
Blaagaard, B. and M. M. Roslyng. (2016). 'Networking the political. On the dynamic interrelations that creates publics in the digital age. *International Journal of Cultural Studies* (November 7): 1–15. https://doi.org/10.1177/1367877916674750.
Blaagaard, B., M. Mortensen and C. Neumayer. (2017). 'Digital images and globalized conflicts'. *Media, Culture and Society* 39(8): 1111–21.
Boudana, S. (2011). 'A definition of journalistic objectivity as performance'. *Media, Culture and Society* 33(3): 385–98.
Braidotti, R. (1991). *Patterns of Dissonance*. Cambridge: Polity.
———. (1994). *Nomadic Subjects*. New York: Columbia University Press.
———. (2006a). 'The becoming-minoritarian of Europe'. In I. Buchanan and A. Parr (eds.), *Deleuze and the Contemporary World* (pp. 79–94). Edinburgh: Edinburgh University Press.
———. (2006b). *Transpositions*. Cambridge: Polity.
———. (2011). *Nomadic Theory*. New York: Columbia University Press.
———. (2013a). *The Post-Human*. Cambridge: Polity.
———. (2013b). 'Becoming-World'. In R. Braidotti, P. Hanafin and B. Blaagaard (eds.), *After Cosmopolitanism* (pp. 8–27). New York/London: Routledge.
———. (2016). 'Don't agonize, organize!' *e_flux conversations*. Retrieved 29 November 2017 from https://conversations.e-flux.com/t/rosi-braidotti-don-t-agonize-organize/5294.
Braidotti, R., P. Hanafin and B. Blaagaard. (2013). *After Cosmopolitanism*. London/New York: Routledge.
Bruns, A. (2008). *Blogs, Wikipedia, Second Life, and Beyond: From Production to Produsage*. New York: Peter Lang.
Butler, J. (1993). *Bodies That Matter*. New York/London: Routledge.
———. (2009). *Frames of War*. London/New York: Verso.
Carey, J. W. (1992). *Communication as Culture*. New York/London: Routledge.
Chakrabarty, D. (2000). *Provincializing Europe. Postcolonial Thought and Historical Difference*. Princeton, NJ: Princeton University Press.
Chouliaraki, L. (2013a). *The Ironic Spectator*. Cambridge: Polity.
———. (2013b). 'Re-mediation, inter-mediation, trans-mediation: The cosmopolitan trajectories of convergent journalism'. *Journalism Studies* 14(2): 267–83.
———. (ed.). (2012). *Self-Mediation: New Media, Citizenship and Civil Selves*. New York/London: Routledge.

Couldry, N. (2008). 'Mediatization or mediation? Alternative understandings of the emergent space of digital storytelling'. *New Media and Society* 10(3): 373–91.

———. (2010). *Why Voice Matters: Culture and Politics after Neoliberalism*. London: Sage.

Curran, J., N. Fenton and D. Freedman. (eds.). (2012). *Misunderstanding the Internet*. London/New York: Routledge.

Dahlgren, P. (2009). *Media and Political Engagement*. Cambridge: Cambridge University Press.

Deleuze, G. (1989). *Cinema 2: The Time-Image*. London: Athlone Press.

Deleuze, G., and F. Guattari. (1994). *What Is Philosophy?* London/New York: Verso.

———. (2004 [1980]). *A Thousand Plateaus*. London/New York: Continuum.

Dencik, L., A. Hintz and J. Cable. (2016). 'Towards data justice? The ambiguity of anti-surveillance resistance in political activism'. *Big Data and Society* 3(2). https://doi.org/10.1177/2053951716679678.

Derrida, J. (1996). *Archive Fever. A Freudian Impression*. Translated by E. Prenowitz. Chicago/London: University of Chicago Press.

Downing, J. D. H. (ed.). 2011. *Encyclopedia of Social Movements*. Thousand Oaks, CA: Sage.

Evans, L. (2009). 'The Black Atlantic: Exploring Gilroy's legacy'. *Atlantic Studies* 6(2): 255–68.

Evans, I. (2016, July 22). 'I wasn't afraid: I took a stand in Baton Rouge because enough is enough'. *The Guardian*. Retrieved 19 October 2017 from https://www.theguardian.com/commentisfree/2016/jul/22/i-wasnt-afraid-i-took-a-stand-in-baton-rouge-because-enough-is-enough.

Fenton, N. (2012). 'The internet and radical politics'. In J. Curran, N. Fenton and D. Freedman'. *Misunderstanding the Internet* (pp. 149–76). London/New York: Routledge.

Fine, R. (2007). *Cosmopolitanism*. London/New York: Routledge.

Foucault, M. (1977). *Discipline and Punish: The Birth of the Prison*. Translated by A. Sheridan. London/New York: Penguin Books.

———. (1982). 'Technologies of the self'. In Paul Rabinow (ed.), *Michel Foucault: Ethics – subjectivity and truth* (pp. 223–51). London/New York: Penguin.

Fraser, N. (1990). 'Rethinking the public sphere: A contribution to the critique of actually existing democracy'. *Social Text* 25(26): 56–80.

Freire, P. (1996). *Pedagogy of the Oppressed*. New York: Bloomsbury.

Friedland, L., and N. Kim. (2009). 'Citizen journalism'. In C. H. Sterling (ed.), *Encyclopedia of Journalism* (pp. 298–302). Thousand Oaks, CA: Sage.

Frosh, P., and A. Pinchevski. (2011). *Media Witnessing: Testimony in the Age of Mass Communication*. London: Palgrave-Macmillan.

Fuchs, C. (2014). *Social Media. A Critical Introduction*. London: Sage.

Gillmor, D. (2004). *We the Media: Grassroots Journalism by the People, for the People*. Sebastopol, CA: O'Reilly.

Gilroy, P. (1987). *There Ain't No Black in the Union Jack*, London: Unwind Hyman.

———. (1991). 'Sounds authentic: Black music, ethnicity, and the challenge of a "changing" same'. *Black Music Research Journal* 11(2): 111–36.

———. (1993). *The Black Atlantic*. London/New York: Verso.

———. (1994). *Small Acts*. London: Serpent's Tail.

———. (2004). *After Empire*. London/New York: Routledge.

Glissant, É. (2007). *Poetics of Relation*. Translated by B. Wing. Ann Arbor: University of Michigan Press.

Goldberg, D. (2002). *The Racial State*. Malden, MA/Oxford: Blackwell.

Gonzáles, J., and J. Torres. (2011). *News for All the People*. New York/London: Verso.

Gøbel, E. (2017). 'David Hamilton Jackson – en vestindisk arbejderleder'. *Personalhistorisk Tidsskrift*, 15–36.
Habermas, J. (1989). *The Structural Transformation of the Public Sphere*. Translated by T. Burger and F. Lawrence. Cambridge: Polity.
———. (2009). 'Media, markets and consumers: The quality press as the backbone of the political public sphere'. In J. Habermas, *Europe: The Faltering Project*. Translated by C. Cronin (pp. 131–37). Cambridge: Polity.
Hampton, M. (2008). 'The "objectivity" ideal and its limits in 20th century British journalism'. *Journalism Studies* 9(4): 477–93.
Hannerz, U. (1996). *Transnational Connections*. New York/London: Routledge.
Haraway, D. (1988). 'Situated knowledges: The science question in feminism as a site of discourse on the privilege of partial perspective'. *Feminist Studies* 14(3): 575–99.
Hariman, R., and J. L. Lucaites. (2007). *No Caption Needed: Iconic Photographs, Public Culture, and Liberal Democracy*. Chicago: University of Chicago Press.
Hartley, J. (2012). 'Silly Citizenship'. In L. Chouliaraki (ed.), *Self-Mediation: New Media, Citizenship and Civic Selves* (pp. 9–24). London/New York: Routledge.
Held, D. (2004). *Global Covenant. The Social Democratic Alternative to the Washington Consensus*. Cambridge: Polity.
Hoxcer Jensen, P. (1981). 'Den Danske vestindiske arbejderbevægelse og strejken i 1916'. *Meddelelser om Forskning i Arbejderbevægelsens Historie Nr. 16 maj*. Copenhagen, Denmark: SFAH.
Isin, E. (2002). *Being Political*. Minneapolis: University of Minnesota Press.
———. (2012). *Citizens without Frontiers*. New York: Bloomsbury.
Isin, E., and E. Ruppert. (2015). *Being Digital Citizens*. Lanham, MD: Rowman & Littlefield.
Isin, E., and G. Nielsen. (eds.). (2008). *Acts of Citizenship*. London/New York: Zed Books.
Jenkins, H. (1992). *Textual Poachers: Television Fans and Participatory Culture*. New York/London: Routledge.
———. (1988). 'Star trek rerun, reread, rewritten: Fan writing as textual poaching'. *Critical Studies in Mass Communication* 5(2): 85–107.
———. (2006). *Convergence Culture*. New York: New York University Press.
———. (2009). 'What happened before YouTube?' In J. Burgess and J. Green (eds.), *YouTube: Online Video and Participatory Culture* (pp. 109–25). Cambridge: Polity. Retrieved 27 May 2014 from http://gossettphd.org/library/jenkins_youtube.pdf.
Jensen, K. Brun. (Ed). (1997). *Dansk Media Historie*. Copenhagen, Denmark: Samleren.
Kaid, L. Lee, and C. Holtz-Bacha (eds.). (2008). *Encyclopedia of Political Communication*. Thousand Oaks, CA: Sage.
King, R. H. (2014). 'Traditions, genealogies, and influences: Gilroy's intellectual routes and roots'. In R. Rutledge Fischer and J. Garcia (eds.), *Retrieving the Human: Reading Paul Gilroy* (pp. 3–30). Albany: State University of New York Press.
Kraidy, M. M. (2016). *The Naked Blogger of Cairo. Creative Insurgency in the Arab World*. Cambridge, MA: Harvard University Press.
Lewis, J., S. Inthorn, and K. Wahl-Jørgensen. (2007). *Citizens or Consumers? What the Media Tell Us about Political Participation*. New York: Open University Press.
Lorde, A. (2007 [1978]). 'Uses of the erotic'. In *Sister Outsider: Essays and Speeches* (pp. 53–59). Berkeley, CA: Crossing Press.
———. (2007 [1979]). 'The master's tools will never dismantle the master's house'. In *Sister Outsider: Essays and Speeches* (pp. 110–13). Berkeley, CA: Crossing Press.
Lott, T. (1994). 'Black cultural politics: An interview with Paul Gilroy'. *Found Object* 4 (Fall): 46–81.
Lunt, P., and S. Livingstone. (2013). 'Media studies' fascination with the concept of the public sphere: Critical reflections and emerging debates'. *Media, Culture and Society* 35(1): 87–96.

Mirzoeff, N. (2011). *The Right to Look: A Counterhistory of Visuality*. Durham, NC: Duke University Press.
———. (2015). *How to See the World*. New York: Basic Books.
———. (2017a). *The Appearance of Black Lives Matter*. Miami, FL: Name Publications.
———. (2017b). 'The historical failure and revolutionary potential of taking a knee'. *Hypoallergic*. Retrieved 19 October 2017 from https://hyperallergic.com/402937/the-historical-failure-and-revolutionary-potential-of-taking-a-knee/.
Morozov, E. (2011). *The Net Delusion: How Not to Liberate the World*. London: Penguin Books.
Mortensen, M. (2017). 'Constructing, confirming, and contesting icons: The Alan Kurdi imagery appropriated by #humanitywashedashore, Ai Weiwei, and Charlie Hebdo'. *Media, Culture and Society* 39(8): 1142–61.
Neumayer, C., and Rossi, L. (2016). '15 years of protest and media technologies scholarship: A sociotechnical timeline. *Social Media+ Society* 2(3). doi:2056305116662180.
Nielsen, P. (2016). *Fru Jensen og andre vestindiske danskere*. Copenhagen, Denmark: Nationalmuseets Forlag.
Olwig, K. Fog. (1993). *Global Culture, Island Identity: Continuity and Change in the Afro-Caribbean Community of Nevis*. Amsterdam, The Netherlands: Harwood Academic Publishers.
Papacharissi, Z. (2015). 'We have always been social'. *Social Media + Society* 1: 1–2.
Patton, P. (2006). 'The event of colonisation'. In I. Buchanan and A. Parr (eds.), *Deleuze and the Contemporary World* (pp. 108–24). Edinburgh: Edinburgh University Press.
Pérez-González, L., B. Blaagaard and M. Baker (eds.). (forthcoming 2019). *The Routledge Encyclopedia of Citizen Media*. New York/London: Routledge.
Peters, C., and M. Broersma (eds.). (2013). *Rethinking Journalism. Trust and Participation in a Transformed News Landscape*. New York/London: Routledge.
Raiford, L. Renee. (2011). *Imprisoned in a Luminous Glare: Photography and the African American Freedom Struggle*. Chapel Hill: University of North Carolina Press.
Rantanen, T. (2003). 'The new sense of place in the 19th-century news'. *Media, Culture and Society* 25: 435–49.
———. (2007). 'Cosmopolizing the news'. *Journalism Studie* 8(6): 843–60.
Rao, S., and H. Wasserman. (2007). 'Global media ethics revisited: A postcolonial critique'. *Global Media and Communication* 3(1): 29–50.
Rettberg, J. Walker. (2014). *Seeing Ourselves through Technology*. Basingstoke, UK: Palgrave Macmillan.
Rich, A. (1984). 'Notes towards a politics of location'. In *Blood, Bread and Poetry* (pp. 210–31). New York: W.W. Norton and Co.
Robinson, A., and S. Tormey. (2010). 'Living in smooth space: Deleuze, postcolonialism and the subaltern'. In S. Bignall and P. Patton (eds.), *Deleuze and the Postcolonial* (pp. 20–40). Edinburgh: Edinburgh University Press.
Rodriguez, C. (2011). *Citizens' Media against Armed Conflict: Disrupting Violence in Colombia*. Minneapolis: University of Minnesota Press.
Rojas, H., and N. Kim. (2008). 'Citizen journalism'. In L. Lee Kaid and C. Holtz-Bacha (eds.), *Encyclopedia of Political Communication* (pp. 106–7). Thousand Oaks, CA: Sage.
Rosen, J. (2008). 'A most useful definition of citizen journalism'. Retrieved 11 March 2016 from http://archive.pressthink.org/2008/07/14/a_most_useful_d.html.
Rothberg, M. (2009). *Multidirectional Memory*. Stanford, CA: Stanford University.
Said, E. (1994). *Representation of the Intellectual. The 1993 Reith Lectures*. New York: Vintage Books.

Schudson, M. (1978). *Discovering the News: A Social History of American Newspapers*. New York: Basic Books.

———. (2003). *The Sociology of News*. New York: W. W. Norton.

Schudson, M., and C. Anderson. (2009). 'Objectivity, professionalism and truth seeking in journalism'. In K. Wahl-Jørgensen and T. Hanitzsch (eds.), *The Handbook of Journalism Studies* (pp. 88–102). New York: Routledge.

Shome, R. (2009). 'Postcolonial studies and communication studies. Mapping new terrains of investigation'. *Journal of Global Mass Communication* 2(3–4): 8–17.

Shome, R., and R. S. Hegde. (2002). 'Postcolonial approaches to communication: Charting the terrain, engaging the intersections'. *Communication Theory* 12(3): 249–70.

Silverstone, R. (2007). *Media and Morality: The Rise of the Mediapolis*. Cambridge: Polity.

Singer, J. B., A. Hermida, D. Domingo, A. Heinonen, S. Paulussen, T. Quandt, Z. Reich and M. Vujnovic. (2011). *Participatory Journalism: Guarding Open Gates at Online Newspapers*. Malden, MA: Wiley-Blackwell.

Spivak, G. C. (1988). 'Can the subaltern speak?' In C. Nelson and L. Grossberg (eds.), *Marxism and the Interpretation of Culture* (pp. 271–313). Urbana: University of Illinois Press.

Starr, P. (2004). *The Creation of the Media: Political Origins of Modern Communications*. Cambridge, MA: Basic Books.

Stephens, M. (1988). *A History of News: From the Drum to the Satellite*. New York/London: Penguin Books.

Sterling, C. H. (ed.). (2009). *Encyclopedia of Journalism*. Thousand Oaks, CA: Sage.

Tuchman, G. (1972). 'Objectivity as strategic ritual: An examination of newsmen's notion of objectivity'. *American Journal of Sociology* 77(4): 660–79.

Tufekci, Z. (2014). 'Is the internet good or bad? Yes'. *Matter*. Retrieved 9 April 2014 from https://medium.com/matter/76d9913c6011.

van Dijck, J. (2013). *The Culture of Connectivity*. Oxford: Oxford University Press.

van Dijck, J., and T. Poell. (2014). 'Constructing public space: Global perspectives on social media and popular contestation'. *International Journal of Communication* 10: 226–34.

van Zoonen, L., F. Vis and S. Mihelj. (2010). 'Performing citizenship on YouTube: Activism, satire and online debate around the anti-Islam video Fitna'. In Lilie Chouliaraki (ed.), *Self-Mediation: New Media, Citizenship and Civic Selves* (pp. 25–38). New York/London: Routledge.

van Zoonen, L. (2005). *Entertaining the Citizen*. Lanham, MD: Rowman & Littlefield.

Wahl-Jørgensen, K. (2012). 'Subjectivity and story-telling in journalism'. *Journalism Studies* 14(3): 1–16.

Wall, M. (2015). 'Citizen journalism: A restrospective on what we know, an agenda for what we don't'. *Digital Journalism* 3(6): 797–813.

Ward, S. J. A. (2008). *The Invention of Journalism Ethics. The Path to Objectivity and Beyond*. Montreal: McGill-Queen's University Press.

Warner, M. (2002). 'Publics and counter publics'. *Public Culture* 14(1): 49–90.

Winant, H., R. Reid-Pharr, M. Rothberg, N. Edwards and T. Lott. (1994). 'Across the Black Atlantic'. *Found Object* 4(Fall): 1–81.

Zarzycka, M. (2012). 'Madonnas of warfare, angels of poverty: Cutting through press photography'. *Photographies* 5(1): 71–85.

Zelizer, B. (2010). *About to Die*. New York: Oxford University Press.

Index

#metoo, 111, 112, 116, 117

activism, 12–13, 16–18, 61, 96, 105, 107, 109, 111, 116
act(s) of citizenship, 9, 34–35, 37, 39, 41–43, 45, 52, 61, 67, 114
aesthetics, 31, 43, 91
affective, 6, 31, 40, 60, 70, 95, 109
affectivity, 5–6, 43
affirmation, 15, 75, 97, 113
affirmative act, 34, 72
agonism, 31–32, 74, 114
Allan, Stuart, 4, 5, 8, 26, 47, 60, 66
America/nism, 90–92, 95–96
Americanism, 53, 55, 64n8, 81, 84–86, 88, 90, 92–93
Anderson, Benedict, 6, 23, 24, 36, 37, 42, 60
archives, 10, 67–71, 80, 84, 86, 87n1, 112
archivization, 11, 69–72, 76, 79, 86–87, 91, 104, 112
Arendt, Hannah, 10, 31, 89
Associated Press, 100
Austin, J. L., 14, 25
authenticity, 5, 6, 73, 104

Bachman, Jonathan, 100
Baker, Mona, 4, 7, 74, 105–6
Balibar, Etienne, 19, 24–26, 35–37, 114
becoming, 13–15, 18–19, 25, 89, 109–13, 116;

becoming-citizen, 25, 43;
becoming-minoritarian, 13, 15–18, 74–75, 95, 108, 110, 113
Benhabib, Seyla, 19, 24, 26, 31, 40–42
Bhabha, Homi, 102, 110, 113–14
Bignall, Simone, 15, 16
Black Atlantic, the, 17, 63, 72–73, 113–14
Black Lives Matter, 11, 90–92, 94–96, 99–101, 110–12, 116
Bough, Ralph J., 62
Braidotti, Rosi, 3, 10–13, 16–20, 34, 39, 46, 58, 60, 70–76, 91, 95, 108, 110–11, 113, 116
Brown, Michael, 95–96, 99, 102–3
Butler, Judith, 25, 34, 90, 94, 97, 116

Carey, James W., 6, 9, 57–58, 60
changing same, the, 10, 70, 73–76, 80, 92, 104–5
Chakrabarty, Dipesh, 19, 20, 24, 93
Chouliaraki, Lilie, 7, 8, 25, 31–34, 43, 59, 66, 89, 106
citizen, the, 2, 14, 20, 24–27, 29, 33–36, 39, 43, 47, 52, 91, 103, 107–9, 114–16;
citizen journalism, 1–13, 16–17, 19–21, 25, 26, 30, 34, 38–40, 42–43, 45–47, 53, 59, 60, 63, 67, 71, 85, 91–93, 96, 103–16;
citizen media, 4, 7, 8, 59, 74, 105;
citizen witnessing, 5;

the citizen subject, 25, 36, 37, 90, 92, 94, 103;
citizens' media, 7, 8
citizenship, theories of, 1, 20;
  citizenship, mediated. *See also* mediated public, 25, 30, 32–33;
  citizen(ship), performative, 33, 34, 35, 52. *See also* performative publicness, performative publics
civil rights, 2, 9–11, 19, 21, 24–25, 51, 53, 56, 61–63, 67, 76, 79, 83–84, 86, 91, 98, 108, 116;
  civil rights movement, 14, 40, 46, 62, 63, 86, 90, 91, 96, 111
colonial society, 45, 50
colonialism, 16, 55, 66, 92
Colored American Review (newspaper), 77
community, 3, 5–7, 9–11, 13–14, 19, 31, 36–37, 42, 49–50, 53, 56, 58, 60–63, 71, 76, 80, 87ff, 89, 107–8, 113, 117;
  community, cosmopolitan, 56, 63;
  community, imaginary, 60
conceptual personae, 3, 12–13, 20
conceptual practice, 2–4, 8, 11–13, 91, 109, 113, 116
connectivity, 6, 39, 46, 57–60
convergence, 27
convergence culture, 60
Copenhagen, 14, 45–46, 49–52, 62–64n1, 67–68
cosmopolitan, 14, 21, 24, 25, 37, 38–42, 46, 51, 56–63, 67, 86, 91, 111, 113
cosmopolitanism, 18, 20, 38–39, 41, 46, 58, 60, 62–63, 86–87n1
Couldry, Nick, 7–8, 31
counter-discourse, 50
counter-memory, 21, 71, 74–75, 92, 96, 111
counter-narrative(s), 42, 59, 70
counter-reading, 2, 11–14, 17, 20, 96, 115
counter-subject, 72, 74
counterpublic, 9–10, 21, 30–31, 34–36, 45–46, 49–52, 55–56, 67, 74, 83, 91, 93
creativity, 18, 20–21, 29, 58, 70, 75–76, 83, 86, 95, 110

The Crisis (newspaper), 51, 54, 62
cultural citizenship, 28
cultural cosmopolitanism, 46
cultural memory, 63, 64n2, 69–70, 86

Dahlgren, Peter, 26, 30, 35
de Certeau, Michel, 61,
de Chabert, Ralph, 76, 77
The Declaration of Independence, 53, 71, 81, 83–86, 87n9, 92, 96, 104
Deleuze, Gilles, 1, 3–4, 12–13, 15–17, 18–20, 32, 42, 72, 74, 113
deliberation, 27, 28, 29, 30, 41, 43, 48, 62, 98, 100, 116;
  deliberation, space of, 28, 52
democracy, 27–28, 52–53, 64n8, 81–82, 88, 92–93, 96, 100–1, 103–4, 116;
  democratic, 5–6, 26–30, 38, 41–42, 48, 56, 90, 94, 96–97
Denmark, 2, 19–20, 40, 45, 48–49, 51–52, 54–55, 58, 62–64n1, 68–70, 76, 80, 83–84, 87nn2–8, 93
Derrida, Jacques, 15, 69–71, 76
deterritorialization, 12–14, 17, 41–43, 54, 72, 90–91, 95, 110;
  deterritorializing, 13, 34, 74, 91
Dewey, John, 5, 7
digital media, 2, 8, 10, 27, 39, 103, 115
Du Bois, W.E.B., 54, 61

embodied expressions, 10;
  embodied politics, 93, 12;
  embodied practice, 2, 12, 57;
  embodiment, 10–11, 25, 32–33, 35, 72, 83, 97, 105;
  embodiedness, 63, 74, 82, 107
Eurocentrism, 3
Evans, Iesha, 101
event, 1, 12–15, 19, 23, 67, 86, 89, 112, 115

Fenton, Natalie, 6, 33
Foucault, Michel, 4, 15, 16, 17, 25, 26, 32, 33, 36, 37, 44n1, 70, 90
Fourth of July, 67, 76, 90
Fraser, Nancy, 9, 29–31, 34, 39, 45, 49–50, 61, 74, 94, 116

Index

Freire, Paulo, 16, 17, 29

gesture, 10, 13, 15, 72, 87, 92, 96, 99–103, 110
Gillmor, Dan, 6, 39
Gilroy, Paul, 10, 14, 17–18, 36, 41, 44n4, 63, 70–76, 92, 104, 113–14
Glissant, Edouard, 17, 74, 87n5
Goldberg, David T., 24–25, 66, 93
Gonzáles, Juan, 6, 51, 58, 66, 94, 97

Habermas, Jürgen, 10, 20, 25–26, 28–30, 43, 66, 98, 116
habitat of meaning, 40
Hannerz, Ulf, 24, 26, 39–42
Hariman, Robert, 10, 96–100, 103
Hartley, John, 27, 28, 29, 32, 33
The Herald (newspaper), 2, 9, 10, 12, 14, 16, 18–26, 35–40, 43, 45–57, 59–64, 66–71, 76–77, 79–81, 83–86, 87nn8–9, 91–94, 104, 110, 112, 115–16
historicity, 8, 21, 73–74, 87, 104, 111

icon, 72, 96–99, 102–3;
  iconic, 10, 96–99, 101–4, 113;
  iconicity, 98–99, 101–4
identification, 11, 17, 24, 33, 39, 67, 80, 111, 114
identity, 11, 16–17, 19, 23–24, 27–29, 33–34, 36–39, 66, 70, 98, 102, 113–14
images, 4, 10–11, 27–28, 90–92, 95–100, 102, 105–6
imaginary, 12, 24, 36–37, 48, 60, 96
imagination, theatrical, 31–33, 39, 106
internet, the 6, 33
Isin, Engin, 9, 19–21, 24–26, 33–37, 39, 41–42, 45, 49–50, 52, 59, 114

Jackson, David Hamilton, 2, 10, 14, 19–20, 23–26, 35, 37, 39–40, 45–59, 61–63, 67–71, 76–81, 83–87, 87n3, 90–93, 95–96, 101, 104–5, 110, 112
Jefferson, Thomas, 92, 93
Jenkins, Henry, 27, 28, 29, 32, 33, 46, 60, 61, 65

Journalism
  journalism, civic, 4, 39;
  journalism, history of, 43, 66;
  journalism, participatory, 4;
  journalism, professional, 2, 4, 5, 8, 9, 25, 43, 60, 115;
  journalism, theory of, 66;
  journalistic practice, 2, 9, 14, 38, 42, 46, 57, 58, 59, 62, 92, 94, 110–11

Klingen (newspaper), 51
Korsaren (newspaper), 51
Kraidy, Marwan, M., 105

labour movement, 48;
  labour strike, 67, 69, 71, 76, 77, 79, 86;
  labour union, 39, 54, 63, 67, 69, 76–79, 85, 87n4, 96
Lincoln, Abraham, 62
Lippmann, Walter, 5, 7
listening, 7, 16, 31, 43, 70, 108–10
Lorde, Audre, 24, 107–9, 113, 117
Lucaites, John Luis, 10, 96–100, 103

Martin, Trayvon, 99
materialisation, 34, 79, 86,
mediatisation, 7, 47
melancholia, 18, 70, 83, 86
memory, 5, 10, 11, 13, 18, 21, 41, 63, 65, 67, 69–76, 79–80, 83–84, 86, 91, 95–96, 99, 102, 104–5, 111–12, 116;
  memory, collective, 5, 65, 68, 80, 86, 95;
  memory, embodied, 71, 76, 85, 99, 111;
  and creativity, 18, 70, 75–76, 86;
  and imagination, 18, 86, 116
Mirzoeff, Nicholas, 10–11, 89–91, 94–95, 97, 99, 101–3, 105
mnemonic, 2, 10, 67, 70, 74, 104–5

narrative(s), 6, 8, 9, 15–16, 18–21n1, 27, 31, 43, 58–59, 61–62, 64n2, 65–66, 69–71, 75–76, 83, 95, 106, 111, 115
nation-state, 2, 20, 24–26, 36–38, 40, 42–43, 47, 57, 63, 114–15
new media, 9

neo-pragmatism, 33
New York, 14, 40, 45–46, 48–49, 51–52, 56–57, 62–63, 67
The New York Evening Journal (newspaper), 49
The New York Evening Standard (newspaper), 62
The New York Sunday American (newspaper), 77
nomadic, 15, 72;
  nomadism, 15–16

objectivity, 5–6, 9, 16, 38–39, 46, 51, 57–59, 94
The Outlook (newspaper), 61, 62, 77

Papacharissi, Zizi, 61
participation, 2–8, 11, 25–29, 31, 33, 38, 41, 43, 48, 90, 94, 97, 104, 110
The Pathfinder (newspaper), 62
Patton, Paul, 13, 14, 15, 16, 89
the people, 5, 19, 35–37, 48–50, 53–56, 69–70, 76, 78, 82, 84–86, 89, 93–94, 101, 109
performative publicness, 31
performativity, 25, 34, 97
photojournalism, 89, 96, 97, 99, 103, 105
political, the, 3–4, 21, 26, 42, 56, 74–75, 84, 86, 98, 107–8, 110;
  political act, 1, 8–10, 12, 14, 18, 19–21, 25–26, 35, 37, 39–40, 43, 45–46, 50–52, 56, 60–61, 63, 67, 70–71, 74, 76, 80, 83–84, 86–87, 89–92, 98–99, 101–3, 105–6, 108–10, 113–16
politics of location, 1, 3, 11–12, 18, 20–21, 34, 42, 72, 75, 76, 108, 110
Politiken (newspaper), 48
post–humanism, 7, 16
postcolonial, the 2, 10, 18, 38, 66–67, 70, 87, 112–15;
  postcolonial memory, 73;
  postcolonial politics, 113;
  postcolonial theory, 1, 3, 16, 21, 113;
  postcolonialism, 16
poststructuralism, 7, 16, 20, 75;
  poststructuralist, 4, 10, 11, 15, 18–19, 21, 32, 71–72, 76, 97, 108, 113–14

public, a, 7, 9–11, 15, 27–28, 31, 33–34, 45–46, 49–52, 56, 62–63, 67–68, 89, 99, 105, 109–10, 112, 114;
public, participatory, 25, 27, 29–31, 33–35, 38, 60, 101, 106, 108–10, 113, 115;
publics, 10–11, 20, 27, 29, 30–31, 33–34, 38–39, 43, 45, 47, 49, 51–52, 61–62, 66, 74, 107, 115;
publics, performative, 37;
public sphere, 2, 6, 20, 25, 27–31, 38–39, 43, 52, 66, 71, 89, 93–100, 102–4, 115–6

racial politics, 14, 66, 103;
racism, 54, 55, 72
radical politics, 33, 34, 39
Rantanen, Terhi, 26, 42, 46, 57, 59, 60
reterritorialization, 12, 13, 14, 45, 53, 56, 67, 71, 72, 116, 117n2;
  reterritorializing, 55, 111
Rich, Adrienne, 1, 3, 12, 13, 110, 114
Robertson, Jeff, 100
Robinson, Andrew, 15, 16, 17
Rodrìguez, Clemencia, 7
Rosen, Jay, 39, 60
Rothberg, Michael, 18, 34, 68
Ruppert, Evelyn, 9, 24, 26, 35, 36, 45

Said, Edward, 114
Silverstone, Roger, 7, 31, 89
situated, 2, 9–12, 14, 33–34, 40, 43, 60, 62, 67, 82, 86, 89, 103, 107, 108, 111;
  situatedness, 9, 10, 40, 82, 107;
  situated knowledges, 75, 89;
social media, 6, 8, 26, 39, 91, 92
Socialdemokraten (newspaper), 48
space of appearance, 11, 21, 31, 89–91, 94–97, 99, 101–5, 108, 110, 114, 116
Spivak, Gayatri, 4, 15–17, 19–20, 32, 34, 66, 75
St. Croix, 2, 14, 19, 23, 40, 45, 47–49, 52–54, 56–57, 61–62, 64nn1–2, 66–71, 76, 79, 81–86, 92–93, 105
The St. Croix Avis (newspaper), 48
St. John, 2, 23, 45, 57, 64nn1–2, 68

St. Thomas, 2, 23, 45, 49, 57, 64nn1–2, 68
subject, the, 13, 15–19, 24–25, 30, 35–36, 44n1, 52, 54, 73–76, 84, 89, 93, 107, 112–3, 116;
    subjectivity, 2–4, 10, 13–14, 18–21, 26, 31, 41, 45, 60–61, 70–72, 74–76, 79, 91, 104, 109–10, 115;
    subjectivity formation, 1, 3, 8, 14, 16, 19, 21, 26, 43, 72, 76, 80, 91, 94, 104–5, 107–9, 112, 114–6

technologies of the self, 32, 36, 44n1, 113
technology, 4, 6, 7, 19, 27, 38–39, 41–42, 46, 47, 57–58, 61, 67, 70–72, 79, 95, 98
territorialization, 12
territory, 20, 24–25, 29, 35–38, 40, 42–43, 54, 63, 64n5, 80, 84
Tomey, Simon, 15–17
Torres, Joseph, 6, 9, 51, 58, 66, 94, 97
The Truthseeker (newspaper), 51

United States Virgin Islands (USVI), 2, 45, 64n5, 68, 81, 83

van Zoonen, Liesbeth, 9, 28, 29, 32
vernacular culture, 14, 74, 75
visibility, politics of, 10, 89, 91, 95, 96
visuality, 10, 19, 89, 90, 91, 97, 100, 104
voice, 3, 7, 8, 15, 27, 29–34, 43, 46, 55, 58–59, 63, 66, 70–71, 85, 90–91, 94–95, 105, 108–9, 114, 116

Warner, Michael, 9–11, 25, 27, 30, 33, 39, 49–50, 68, 74
Washington, Booker T., 54, 61–62
Wells, Ida B., 51
The West End News (newspaper), 48
whiteness, 17, 97, 103
Wilcox, Ella Wheeler, 62
witness, 5, 10, 71, 102
witnessing, 5, 8, 112;
    witnessing, media, 5

About the Author

Bolette B. Blaagaard is Associate Professor of Communications at Aalborg University, Copenhagen, Denmark. She is the co-editor of *Deconstructing Europe: Postcolonial Perspectives* (2012), *After Cosmopolitanism* (2013), *Cosmopolitanism and the New News Media* (2014) and *Citizen Media and Public Spaces* (2016), among others.

www.ingramcontent.com/pod-product-compliance
Lightning Source LLC
Chambersburg PA
CBHW021833300426
44114CB00009BA/423